Isle of Coll

Facets of a Gem

Ewen McGee

Islands Book Trust

Published in 2015 by the Islands Book Trust

www.theislandsbooktrust.com

ISBN: 978-1-907443-18-3

The author and publishers are grateful to the Estate of Stephen Spender for their kind permission to reproduce a short extract from the poem 'The Truly Great', from New Collected Poems by Stephen Spender ©2004, published by Faber & Faber.

Unfortunately some of the images in this book are of poor quality; these have nevertheless been included, because of their importance to the publication.

Islands Book Trust, Laxay Hall, Laxay,
Isle of Lewis, Eilean Siar, HS2 9PJ.
Tel: 01851 830316

Typeset by Erica Schwarz (www.schwarz-editorial.co.uk)
Cover design by Raspberry Creative Type
Printed and bound by Martins the Printers, Berwick upon Tweed

Contents

May 2011 – Work is under way at the An Cridhe site.

April 2012 – The bunkhouse, at right, and the main An Cridhe building are at an advanced stage.

Early July 2012 – Everything looks about ready for the opening.

Weds 11th July 2012 – The main hall is packed as an attentive crowd hears Her Royal Highness The Princess Royal declare An Cridhe officially open.

Foreword

In July 2012 I was delighted to be asked to open the new An Cridhe. Its popularity reflects the strength of island society. This book tells some of the stories which illustrate the history which has contributed to the thriving community on this Island of Coll. Its history and people go back a very long way and there are many stories to tell. My knowledge is much more recent but this book will add greatly to my meagre store. I hope this book will interest and entertain those who already know and or live on Coll and those who have yet to have that pleasure. I suspect that it may also flush out some more chapters!

Thank you to Ewen McGee for your diligent searching and time consuming creation of this fascinating book.

Her Royal Highness The Princess Royal

July 2014

Heard at the back of the wall:
"What's happening now?"
"Maybe signing up for life membership of the island sailing club."
"As a tutor?"

July 2012 – An Cridhe is a flexible building, with a number of rooms. The main hall is marked out for badminton, but can host concerts, plays, etc.

Thurs 12th July 2012 – The main hall is packed again, for more VIPs...

Thurs 12th July 2012
~~Phil and Ali~~ – Ali and Phil entertain the crowd with jokes and, 'occasionally', music.

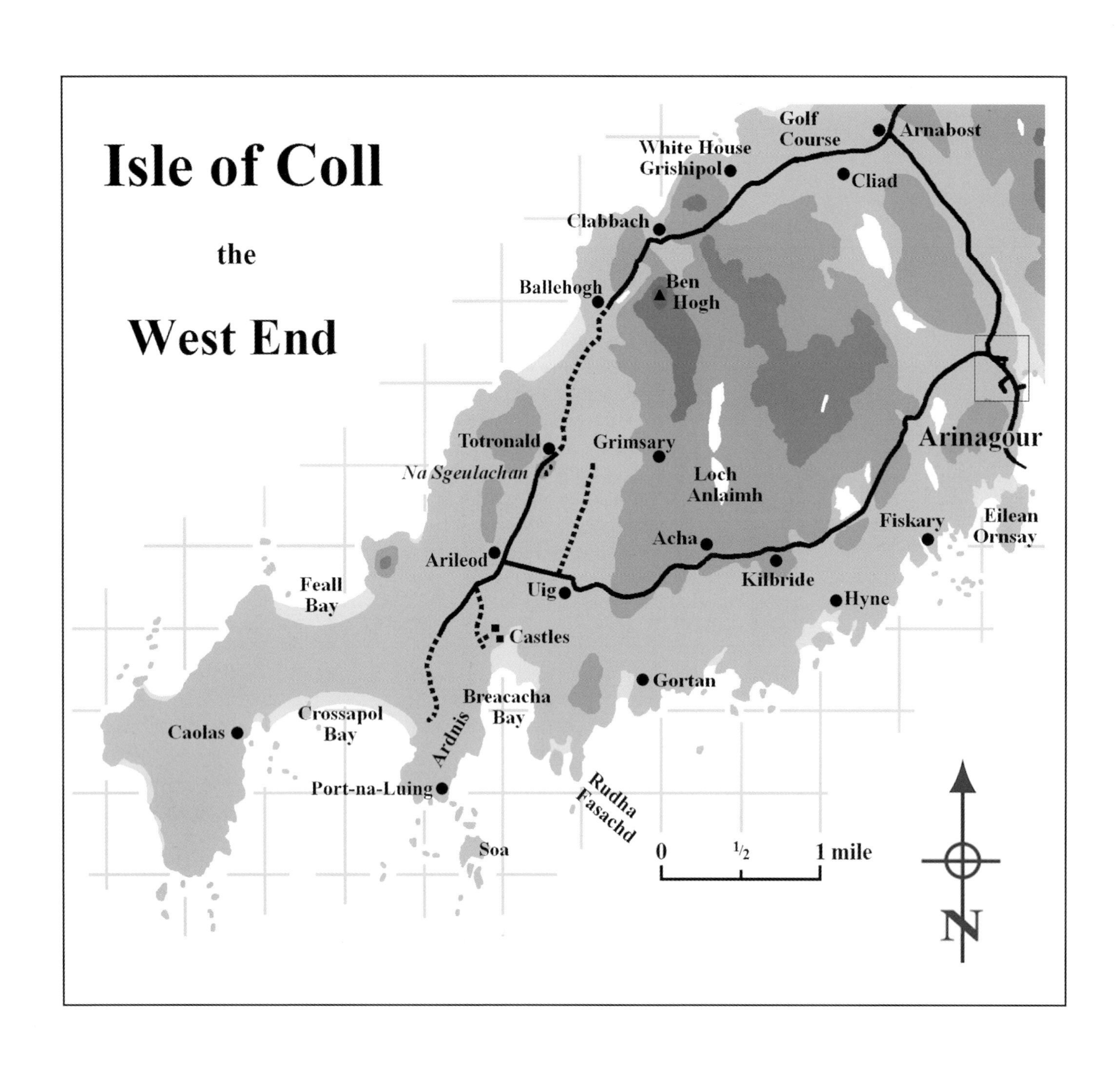

Isle of Coll
the
West End
Golf
Course
Arnabost
White House
Grishipol
Cliad
Clabbach
Ballehogh
Ben
Hogh
Totronald
Grimsary
Arinagour
Na Sgeulachan
Loch
Anlaimh
Fiskary
Eilean
Ornsay
Acha
Arileod
Kilbride
Feall
Bay
Uig
Hyne
Castles
Gortan
Breacacha
Bay
Crossapol
Bay
Caolas
Ardnis
Port-na-Luing
Rudha
Fasachd
Soa
0
1/2
1 mile
N

Introduction

"Coll? Where's that?"

AN OFTEN-ASKED question: "Coll? Where's that?" The time has come to rectify this sad lack of knowledge in some quarters and these pages hold stories from, and the history of, this Hebridean gem. Na Sgeulachan (the Tellers of Tales, the island's two best-known standing stones) would tell us everything there is to know if only they had not fallen silent. Still, there are very many written works to fall back on: newspaper articles and adverts, books, booklets, official records, correspondence, websites, minutes of meetings, and so on. Not the least of the written works are the journals of Dr Samuel Johnson and his companion James Boswell who spent ten days on the island in 1773. In fact, such a large amount of material is available about Coll and its people that these pages only tell a small part – maybe more 'volumes' need to follow at a later date? Any account though would be incomplete without some of the tales that have been told in front of a peat fire, and you may imagine that many of these would have had the company in tears of laughter. Sadly, all the storytellers cannot be given due credit – here we need to reverse the old maxim and say that probably everyone is guilty until proven innocent, especially when it comes to the likes of the 'plunder' of the *Nevada*. There are some points to note:

- The three piers in Loch Eatharna (Arinagour Bay) are referred to throughout as the old pier (nearest the hotel), the middle pier, and the new pier (really long one).
- Place names will generally refer to locations on Coll unless stated otherwise.

➤

Na Sgeulachan (the Tellers of Tales)

Tourist Tip:

You've come ashore without an overnight bag and change of clothing? Better be back down at the pier in plenty of time for the second and last boat of the day – assuming, of course, that it's what is referred to as a 'two-boat' day. You know, people have landed on the island to do something as basic as fixing a dripping tap and have never left – and, no, they weren't kidnapped! Better still, why not stay one night at least, because at the end of 2013 Coll was awarded the status of Dark Sky Community by the International Dark-Sky Association.

- Spelling of forenames, surnames and locations is very much as shown on original documents but, where it is considered helpful, alternative spelling is included.
- Lastly, the reader may suspect that the book has a distinctly nautical bias. Well, we *are* talking about an island. So, sit back and relax, and discover the facets of this gem. Then, head out and step ashore!

Chapter 1

F. Flintstone & Co.

Ask why God made the gem so small,
And why so huge the granite?
Because God meant mankind should set
That higher value on it.

Robert Burns 1759–1796

WHERE shall we start? Creation seems as good a point as anywhere, even for what is just a short history lesson. It is said that after God had finished his work in six days He found there was a bag of jewels left over. Rather than working on the seventh day, He just opened a window in heaven and dropped them out. The *Coll* version of the story, concocted purely for this book, goes on to explain that the rough diamonds were strewn by the wind on the way down and formed all the other islands such as Mull, Skye, the Outer Hebrides, etc. But one perfect gem made a perfect landing at a point 56 degrees 39 minutes north of the equator, and 6 degrees 32 minutes west of a line of longitude which ran through a point to be known later as Greenwich. And now you know *where* Coll is, but the *when* of this historical event is another matter. As we shall see, dates are quite imprecise until we reach the last few hundred years or so.

The rock of this gem is Lewisian gneiss, one of the oldest rocks in Europe and dating from 3,000 to 4,000 million years ago. To clarify things, maybe, this gneiss is a banded or foliated metamorphic rock consisting mainly of feldspar, quartz and mica. More recently – and talking in terms of thousands rather than millions of years – the hills of Coll were shaped by glaciation and huge boulders ended up looking as if randomly scattered across the landscape, like the one that sits perched on three small stones at the top of Ben Hogh. Somewhat younger than the gneiss is the dark basalt which appears in narrow strips or 'dykes'. Coll's other minerals include white quartzite, dark red garnets, some marble, and two small veins of lead.

Turning from the hard stuff to something softer, we find that Coll was given lovely machair in abundance. Machair is a very rare feature and nearly all of it is found on the Atlantic coast of Scotland. It has developed from shellfish whose shells have been pounded by storms, grinding them down and so allowing them to be blown inland. This shell sand helps to create the machair, since it is alkaline and neutralises the acid from the peaty soil. The result is a landscape that is fertile and for a few weeks each summer there is a spectacular carpet of wild flowers. The shell sand also provided Coll with over twenty golden beaches, from the small and medium to a back-to-back pair about a mile long. Up from the machair and on the rough moorland lie many fresh water lochs, some well-known for their trout and, not so very long ago, salmon still ran in the streams that were fed from these lochs.

Coll must have been shouting to the Creator, "This is all wonderful, but please think of the other islands too." Then its weather was added: frequent days of mainly clear blue skies, and these later began to be recorded by a close neighbour and they often top the UK sunshine records. The wind? It blows most of the time from the south-west and, as a result, the air arrives pure and fresh after a journey of thousands of miles over nothing but open sea. Rain? It is a much needed feature to maintain Coll's fertile soil, and here we must be honest and say that not every day is bone dry. So, should you perchance hear someone say that rain falls just once a year, remember that most people might call that the tourist season.

The first people to set foot on this idyllic location arrived after the covering ice sheet had melted. Archaeologist Steve Mithen has identified Fiskary Bay on Coll as the second oldest known human settlement in the Hebrides, dating it at approximately 7350 to 7050 BC. (Kinloch on the Isle of Rum is dated a few hundred years earlier.) These Mesolithic 'Flintstones' were hunter-gatherers, living on hazelnuts, fish and seals, and wisely they brought the material to make weapons such as their harpoons to catch fish – Coll is devoid of flint.

Much later than the 'Flintstones' came the 'Beaker' people of the Bronze Age, and pieces of their pottery beakers record their presence on Coll about 2000 BC. Also in the Bronze Age, island dwellings appeared on some inland lochs and these were artificial islands known as crannogs. Usually a submerged and twisting causeway was the access route and this offered protection for the island dwellers, since only they would know its location and its shape for making a safe crossing. These crannogs were to be used by different inhabitants over many centuries.

Much later again, the Vikings began raiding in the Hebrides and soon established themselves in the islands. Their presence on Coll provides us with a record of some personal names. The island is mentioned as the headquarters of Earl Gilli, a representative and brother-in-law of Sigurd who ruled the Orkneys and Hebrides about 1000 AD. Secondly, an old Irish poem has the line: 'A Radhnaill a ri Cola' [O Raghnall, O King of Coll] and, hence, Coll's place-name of

Fiskary Bay, Coll, identified as the location of the second oldest known human settlement in the Hebrides, dated at approximately 7350 to 7050 BC. (Photo: E. McGee)

Totronald – or Totaranald. A third name is Gaut – he became quite a famous stonemason on the Isle of Man, where he 'signed' a cross which is dated to about the year 950: 'Gaut made this, son of Bjørn from Kolli [Coll]'. The fourth name is Grim, and MacEchern thinks he may be the origin of the place-name Grimsary (Grim's sheiling). In the *Story of Burnt Njal*, Grim and Helgi are identified as Njal's sons and in the latter part of the 10th century, '… they fared south to Wales, and harried there. Then they held on for [the Isle of] Man, and there they met Godred, and fought with him, and got the victory … north to Coll, and found Earl Gilli there, and he greeted them well, and there they stayed with him a while.'

These Norse invaders occupied a number of Duns, or hill forts, either of their making or the work of earlier settlers. A look at a reasonable scale Ordnance Survey map – say 1:50,000 – will show them all. Dùn an Achaidh, or just Dun Acha, is about the easiest to spot. It is a conspicuous ridge just off to the left of the West End road, not long after you pass Acha and its old mill, as you head west. It is regarded as the best preserved Dun on the island. Tradition tells how they finally lost their hold of Coll, and it was due largely to a man called Lachlan. He arrived at Loch Anlaimh (the lower mill loch) disguised as a musician and was guided by Norsemen over a hidden causeway to their island fort. For some hours he entertained them with music on his clarsach, and then when the chance arose he got hold of their weapons and flung them into the loch. He was to return later with others and they slaughtered the garrison. The end came when all the remaining Norsemen on the island gathered at nearby Grimsary and a battle was fought with the native islanders, the latter proving victorious.

Coll eventually came under the ownership of MacDonald, Lord of the Isles, who granted it to the first McLean of Coll early in the 1400s. That's enough of a history lesson for now.

Chapter 2

NEIGHBOURS

"If you *can't* see Mull very clearly then it's probably raining.
If you *can* see Mull very clearly then it's probably going to rain!"

Anon

WITH Coll being such a great place why should we mention the neighbours at all? Well, there was the recent 'fast food' supply – full story later – but a sensible answer is that some of their inhabitants were to be welcomed as immigrants to add to Coll's population. Quite literally, fresh blood was added to a tight-knit community where almost every person had a fairly close blood relationship to many others. Until such time as Coll had regular and reliable transport connections the population grew mainly through intermarriage. On some occasions, almost inevitably, the bride and groom would be first cousins and such a situation is captured in the comedy movie *The Bridal Path*. The preacher of the story's fictitious island, having just returned from the big city on the mainland and where he has come across a big word that was new to him, does a bit of strong pulpit thumping on the Sunday: "There will be no consanguinity on this island!" And, for his flock in the pews, he clarifies the meaning of the word: "I will have no first cousin marrying first cousin!" It may be of interest that marriage of first cousins, while legal within the UK, is still quite an issue throughout the world. For example, in the USA some states permit such marriages and some don't.

If some incomers were to be welcomed, others were far from friendly and were repelled! To watch out for any invading forces, or simply just to get the best view of as many of Coll's neighbours as possible, one really needs to get a good bit above sea level and it is hard to beat the summit of Ben Hogh, at 339 feet the island's highest hill. The introductions go clockwise: to the northwest lies a distant neighbour, the 'Long Island' (the Outer Hebrides), about forty-two miles away at its closest. On many days the hills are visible and the white buildings of Barra Head lighthouse, over 600 feet above sea level and right at the southern end of the island chain, can sometimes be picked out with binoculars. You may know of *'Ernie, the Fastest Milkman in the West'* (a 1971 hit song), but be as yet unaware of the *'Clansman, the slowest fast food delivery ship in the Hebrides'*. To the Isle of Barra came a chef with a speciality in curries, and his reputation quickly spread – even as far as Coll, over forty miles away. An arrangement soon developed where a bulk order was phoned out to Barra on a Thursday, and the 'goods' were loaded at Castlebay onto the *Clansman*, which had the following schedule:

Depart Barra 15:15
Arrive Tiree 18:00
Depart Tiree 18:15
Arrive Coll 19:10

Let's say that's at least four and a half hours for the 'fast food' from the kitchen on Barra to the hands of the Coll recipients. The food was well packaged and instructions for the re-heating were provided. All went well for a long while, until the story appeared in the national press. Officialdom read the story and officialdom, presumably quoting the relevant regulations, said, "Must stop!"

The Small Isles – Canna, Rum, Muck, Eigg – lie to the north, varying from fourteen to twenty-nine miles away. In the dip between the peaks of Rum, the jagged ridge of the Black Cuillin on the Isle of Skye is often seen, and from a vantage point near Coll's Bealach na Gaoithe (the Windy Gap) the view across a deep blue sea on a sunny day can be quite stunning! The four Small Isles 'lost' a few people in the direction of Coll over the years, but there were links with Coll as far back as the 1600s – the first McLean of Muck was a son of Lachlan McLean, 6th chief of Coll.

Part of the mainland is the odd one out in the circle of neighbours. Ardnamurchan Point with its lighthouse, the most westerly point of the British mainland, stands about nine miles east of Sorisdale. Coll was to know a small amount of intermarriage with incomers from Ardnamurchan and from nearby Morven.

Between east and south-east lie Mull and the Treshnish Isles. Mull is relatively close, about six miles from Coll to Caliach Point, and Ben More at twenty three miles away stands proudly at 3,172 feet to its sharp-pointed summit. The Kilninian Parish on Mull added to Coll's population, sometimes by whole families, sometimes just by a single person. McLean of Coll's Quinish estate lay within Kilninian Parish and the incomers may well have been known as possessing skills which could be put to good use on his Coll estate. Then there is the string of the mostly flat-topped Treshnish Isles: the larger ones such as Fladda and Lunga and, to the south of them, the very distinctive Dutchman's Cap (Bac Mòr). Five miles behind the Treshnish is Staffa, famous for Fingal's Cave, but it is not so easily identified. Low-lying Iona of Saint Columba fame may be visible but can be hard to distinguish from the Ross of Mull. The good Hebridean visibility often allows the very distinctive Paps of Jura to be identified – these three closely-grouped hills are about fifty-three miles away to the south-east.

Finally, to the south-west of Coll is its closest neighbour, the Isle of Gunna, and about twenty miles further to the south-west is the Skerryvore rock with its lighthouse. Between Gunna and Skerryvore there is absolutely nothing! Except Tiree.

Now, does the reader suspect that someone is having a wee dig at Tiree? Never fear, for Tiree is well able to give as good as it gets. The on-going war of words was kept going by Viator when in 1859 he, or she, penned the following article to the Scotsman newspaper:

> ISLAND OF TYREE
>
> October 18, 1859
>
> Sir, – As there is nothing particularly fresh or absorbing at the present moment, perhaps your readers might find some little amusement in taking a glance at the above-named interesting little outpost of Her Majesty's dominions. If ever you should think of paying it a visit, let it be in the summer time. But if chance or necessity should bring you at any other season, put a good water-proof great-coat and a sou'-wester among your luggage …
>
> However unpromising the general aspect of the island, it is nevertheless remarkably fertile. The pasture is rich … The Tyree people are proud of their island, and would not exchange it for any other place. Coll is nothing to it. Everything they have in Tyree – fish, flesh, or fowl – is superior to anything in Coll. They are themselves also superior to the Coll people, at least don't hint anything to the contrary. … – I am, &c.
>
> VIATOR

What Viator wrote about the folk on the Isle of Barra has been omitted in order to avoid an immediate full-scale invasion of Tiree by the MacNeils sailing over in a modern-day version of Kisimul's Galley.

Chapter 3

A Policeman's Lot

IN THE Old Statistical Account of the 1790s it is claimed that there had been no robbery, murder or suicide on Coll – not just for a week, or a year, but for generations! Nevertheless, over more recent decades the number of regulations has grown and grown, and police officers from Mull, Tiree and the mainland have visited Coll, usually just to conduct routine checks. Naturally, the population would wish to know the expected arrival time, in order not to burden the visiting officer with a lot of unnecessary work. If the officer was coming across from Mull then a Collach's cousin in Tobermory might phone over with the information that Sergeant Mc— was observed boarding the *Claymore*. Failing that, there was always the wavelength that the *Claymore*'s radio operator would be broadcasting on.

When the Tiree officers were involved they would usually come over on a local lobster boat which doubled up as a ferry. Landing on Coll somewhere in the West End they would make their way to the nearest house and be offered the use of the phone to call the taxi. After the taxi had collected its passengers the same phone would be put to further good use!

A third and very rare method of arrival was to come ashore in plain clothes. A pair of such officers stepped out of the *Claymore* into the island's red ferry boat and immediately raised some doubts in the minds of the other passengers. The two gents just didn't have that holiday-maker look about them – their smart suits stood out against the more casual wear of other passengers and there was the lack of appropriately labelled and well-used holiday cases. A few minutes later they set foot on the middle pier and 'justified' their trip by identifying that one Collach had broken the law. A vague memory says it was something like an uninsured vehicle. In an instant, the rest of the island – i.e. beyond the bounds of the middle pier – appeared almost miraculously to be as pure as the driven snow.

It would be wrong though to think that the island has always been totally free of crime – there has been the occasional minor infringement. 'Hector' was driving on his own across the island when he came upon a solitary walker on the road. The offer of a lift was accepted and the conversation soon began:

"And what brings you to Coll today?"
"I came over to conduct a driving test."
(Yes, in the good old days they did that on Coll, a place of single-track roads, no traffic lights or pedestrian crossings.)
"Och well, perhaps you could give me a test while you're here then?"

The transcript of the subsequent court proceedings is unfortunately not to hand but it is said that 'Hector' presented a very good defence – something like driving a relative to the airstrip for an air ambulance flight and then forgetting there would be no licensed driver with him in the car on the way back home, and the 'L' plates were forever coming loose what with animals or the state of the road surface, and so on. The outcome: case dismissed!

Chapter 4

Power to the People

"We never know at what time the electricity generating company through the wall will be heading for bed!"

YOU'VE been for a good walk – *off* road – and not on the lovely machair but on the broad, spongy, peaty moorland. Then, without warning, one foot goes deep down into the peat bog and cold muddy water pours into the boot. You're far from being the first person to be caught out like that.

Tourist Tip:

A walking pole is just the thing for testing the ground ahead.

This wonderful Coll peat, of which there is still a plentiful supply, is fine for heating but it is a supply of oil lamps and candles which provided illumination for thousands of years. When the Lord is giving Moses details for the Ark of the Covenant there are very specific directions for making lamps, such as: ' … wick trimmers and trays are to be of pure gold …' [Exodus 25:38]. Fast forward many centuries and, apart from the 'pure gold' bit, probably little had changed by 1773 when Johnson and Boswell visited Coll. They found the islanders making candles from the tallow of their beasts and making oil for their lamps from fish liver.

Then along came pressure oil lamps such as the Tilley and these gave a brighter light, burning happily for a few hours before needing pumped up again. When the Friday night dance in the old village hall

A crusie lamp of the type that had a wick, and burned fish liver oil. The lower bowl is to catch drips from above. (Photo: E. McGee)

stopped around 11 pm for tea and sandwiches, the lamps were unhooked from the roof and given the necessary attention. Come to think of it, in the middle of an energetic Strip-the-Willow dance with arms swinging wildly and bodies sometimes being flung off at a tangent, the only safe place for a burning lamp was high up out of the way.

As far as cooking and heating is concerned, it is only in the past few decades that the use of peat has dwindled away to just a few households. Coll's peat is not only of good quality but it was of such a quantity as to let the neighbours have some. The Old Statistical Account of the 1790s tells us: 'The only peat-moss in the island [of Tiree] which is of very inferior quality … is now nearly exhausted. They are obliged to bring their fuel with great labour and at a heavy expense, some from Mull and some from Coll.'

After peat, coal was the next fuel to come into use on Coll, although the islanders often mixed the two, finding that the combination gave out a better heat while still retaining a good measure of economy. Bottled gas became available in the early 1900s and eventually was to be found on the island where it became popular for cooking and lighting, but places such as the shop and hotel were to benefit also with refrigerators that could operate on gas.

Small 12-volt wind generators enjoyed a period of popularity, but why should the islanders have been denied food mixers, hair dryers, televisions, etc., all needing 240 volts? So, by about 1960 a few properties had a generating unit installed, often in a small lean-to shed. One such unit was the Lister Start-O-Matic, where the wiring was arranged with the generator being effectively controlled by the switches in the house. It started up automatically when the first electrical item was switched on, and stopped when the last item was switched off. Entering a darkened house and switching on the hall light would result in a continued black-out for a second or two. In the background would come the 'chug-a-chug-a-chug' of the unit starting up and the light would rapidly brighten as the engine reached its normal operating rate. Not enough electricity was generated by the Start-o-Matic for power-hungry items like a washing machine or an immersion heater but it was adequate for something like a television. Thus, a household could have spare capacity and one magnanimous family in the village ran a cable through the attic to their next-door neighbours, just for a light in the living room. A late evening visit to these neighbours had an element of entertainment since, from about 9 pm onwards, a match or taper was always kept handy in readiness for lighting the gas mantle: "We never know at what time the electricity generating company through the wall will be heading for bed!"

Eventually, in the 1970s, mains electricity arrived from Tiree's generating station, perhaps a sort of 'thank you' in return for many years of Coll peat. Then, a few years later a cable-laying ship brought a new mains supply ashore at the East End from the mainland via the Isle of Mull, and this supply was run the length of the island right down to the West End and then on across Gunna and Gunna Sound to Tiree.

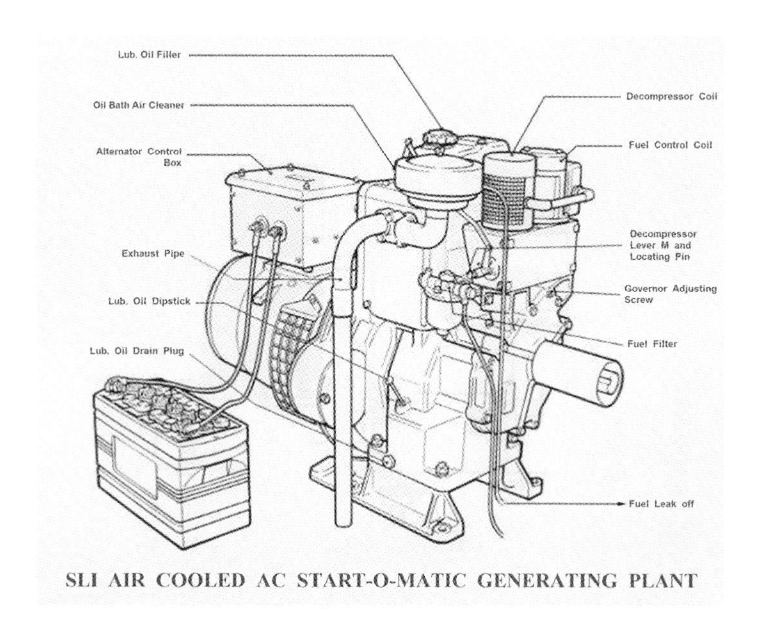

The Lister Start-O-Matic 240-volt generating unit which found favour with some households on Coll. The full set of installation instructions included an electrical wiring diagram.

Jumping back a bit in the history of fuel supplies, the first cars arrived on the island in 1924/25 and with these rose the need for a local petrol outlet. The need was met initially by a 500 gallon tank sited not far from the middle pier – just a short up-hill distance to push the full petrol drums. Later the petrol tank and its hand-operated pump were located next to the Free Church in Arinagour and, even later again, the mains electricity allowed for the pumps you see today adjacent to the war memorial. For a few decades all the fuel arrived in drums on the regular cargo ship, but the Ro-Ro (Roll on, Roll off) ship eventually became the norm and the fuel now arrives by tanker on the ferry. If the price at the pumps causes you to gasp then be aware that it's down to the economy of scale. The tanker is on the road – and the sea – for maybe as much as eight or nine hours and in that time will be able to make only one delivery. On the mainland a good few service stations will have had their tanks replenished in the same time.

Modern technology for heating has been embraced by islanders, especially for new-build houses. There are some properties using the ground source heat pump, and even more recently the air source heat pump has made its mark. Lastly, when considering modern technology, there *are* some wind turbines.

Chapter 5

Mind the Gap

A causeway too far?

THE GAP? This is the 1,400 yard wide Gunna Sound between the Islands of Gunna and Tiree, plus the much narrower and shallower gap from Coll to Gunna, which combine to prevent easy travel between Coll and Tiree. We shall go very nautical for a moment and tell you that the flood stream runs north-west through the Sound and the ebb south-east, at about two and a half to three knots. A very nasty sea gets up if there is a strong wind with an adverse tide. And, if that is not enough, the Sound has a number of hazardous rocks. At low water there is a minimum depth of about thirty feet. The Sound is not used by a large number of vessels, but of importance are the local fishing boats and the summer ferry schedule which includes an Oban-Coll-Tiree-Barra sailing and back once a week. It is also useful to pleasure craft making a passage from Coll or Tiree out to Barra – it does away with a detour north round the Cairns of Coll or south round Skerryvore.

Surprisingly, there is a quite an old written account of a journey across the gap. Necker de Saussure, a Swiss Professor of Mineralogy, had a week's stay on Coll in 1818 and he writes:

> September 3d. We set out to visit the Isle of Tiree. These two isles are separated by a strait of five miles in breadth, [possibly the distance between his Coll departure point and the Tiree arrival point] in the midst of which the little Isle of Guna is situated. Having reached the southern extremity of Coll, we took a small boat which two boatmen drew with great difficulty from the sand in which it was wedged … between Coll and Guna is very narrow, and dangerous, from the quantity of sand-banks and shallow places with which it abounds; and our boatmen were frequently obliged to jump into the water to push the boat from the sand-banks. Having surveyed the Isle of Guna, consisting entirely of rocks of gneiss, we were an hour in reaching Tiree.

On the next day, they left Balephetrish and headed back to the north-east end of Tiree where they '… found a boat ready to cross the strait.'

To make a crossing between Coll and Tiree there was for many years a recognised ferry service operating, but not to any great published timetable. The Coll end was often at Caolas, where there was an inn, but sometimes the landing or departing spot was at Port-na-Luing, where there was also an inn, or maybe near McLean's tomb at the east end of Crossapol beach. The cargo could be livestock such as male calves. Cheese also crossed the gap to Tiree, and the Coll cheese was very famous even to the extent of appearing on the House of Commons dining room menu. At the peak of the industry in 1900, Coll had an output of about sixty tons of cheese a year. Production gradually declined but in the 1930s there were still seven dairy farms with stocks of Ayrshire cows, all engaged in making Cheddar and

Stilton. For the transport of livestock it was important to protect the ferry's timber frames from hooves and this was achieved by a blanket of bracken and heather. This covering on top of a ballast of stones also absorbed the cow dung.

The arrival of larger and faster vessels operating from Oban to Arinagour and then to Scarinish on Tiree brought about the decline of the local ferry and its shorter sea crossing, although it may still be operating today even if in a very an ad-hoc fashion.

In the second half of the 20th century, many of the Hebridean islands found themselves being joined by a causeway to a neighbour: Vatersay to Barra, Eriskay to South Uist, Berneray to North Uist, not to mention the causeways within the Uists themselves. There has also been talk of longer links such as one across the Sound of Harris and possibly even one from Barra to the Uists. So, has any kind of fixed link even been considered for the Coll-Tiree gap? Yes, according to the press in 2001:

> *Will Coll and Tiree be in a fix?*
>
> Islanders on Coll and Tiree were asked about a fixed link between their two islands. Would this help breathe new life into the communities?

The article stemmed from a local authority feasibility study where the Community Councils on both islands were consulted via a questionnaire. They were though advised that a fixed link was not very likely to be established due to environmental considerations and the various replies were, as a result, quite ambivalent. The environmental issues were the degradation of the dune system (new road requirements), disturbance of bird populations and seal breeding, archaeological sites close to likely routes, and more.

Both island communities could see a good number of advantages and disadvantages. Coll would gain access to a daily air link to the mainland and access to a secondary school. It could though lose some of its own trades. Tiree businesses might acquire some Coll customers but saw a danger in Coll becoming the main and only ferry terminal. Both islands envisaged an increase in the number of short-stay visitors and day trippers. A number of fixed-link routes were considered, as was a short ferry crossing, and all had very significant cost implications. Savings were envisaged in the areas of education and community services, but a causeway solution was deemed to have only limited potential in generating electricity.

So, a fixed link – is it a causeway too far, or is it a case of never say 'never'?

An aerial photo showing Coll, Gunna and Tiree. Starting from the foot of the photo we see Coll with the south end of Crossapol beach on the left. Then Caolas Ban between Coll and Gunna, a narrow and very shallow strait. Next, Gunna itself. Above that is 'the Gap' – Gunna sound – looking disproportionally narrow because of the angle of the photograph. Lastly, at the top, Tiree with the large sweeping indentation of Gott Bay on the left. (Photo courtesy of A. Moar)

Chapter 6

ON A WING AND A PAIR

London's Heathrow now onto its fifth terminal?
That's nothing! Coll is now onto its fifth airfield!

PERHAPS the 'Wing' and the 'Pair' should be reversed since the biplane era is usually thought of as preceding that of the monoplane. But, to continue …

The first recorded flight to Coll was a one-off event, and the arrival at Arinagour was more of a splashdown than a touchdown. In the middle of June 1932 there were four flying boats based at Oban for two weeks. These military planes, Supermarine Southamptons, were working with the Scottish fishery fleet and this was to help locate elusive herring shoals in the seas south and west of Tiree, near to Dhu Heartach and Skerryvore. At least one of the four planes was available when an urgent message was received at Oban regarding a patient on Coll, and a local doctor made the journey out to the island in a flight time of twenty-five minutes.

The year 1933 saw the start of air services to the Highlands and Islands by Midland & Scottish Air Ferries. In that year the company ordered some de Havilland Fox Moth biplanes. They were planning to establish a passenger service to Stornoway and the first plane to land on Lewis soil, on an exploratory flight, was one of their Fox Moths. The flight was in June, leaving Renfrew Aerodrome near Glasgow and touching down initially on Coll, making it the first time a plane had actually landed on the island. The Fox Moth then flew out to North Uist, and in the late evening light it arrived over Stornoway and got its wheels safely on the grass just before Saturday turned to Sunday.

Also in 1933, on the 14th May, Midland & Scottish were involved in what is regarded as the first air ambulance flight in Scotland, the transfer of a sick man from the island of Islay to Renfrew. The first such flight to Coll was in the middle of August 1936, with the grouse season just three days old. One party of visitors was reported as '… enjoying good sport, and returning good bags shooting.' Unfortunately, the 'good sport' included the accidental shooting (in the foot!) of an eighteen-year old gillie, Johnnie MacInnes of Bousd. Captain J. A. Hankins of Northern & Scottish Airways was on Skye with his aircraft when he received a radio message with news of the incident. He flew his three-engined Spartan Cruiser over to Coll, coping with poor visibility on the way, and landed on the beach below the castles. There was a little wait while the injured lad was brought the few miles to Breacacha, but soon Johnnie was in the air on his way to Renfrew and then on by road to Glasgow's Western Infirmary.

With the outbreak of the 1939–45 war and with the need for an airfield quite independent of tides, a stretch of grass at Feall became an emergency landing ground. A very large conspicuous stone nearby had a Royal Air Force roundel painted on top to act as a marker. Even after such a passage of time, a few flaky remnants of the paint are still visible today, as is a bolt cemented on top and which held down the windsock.

After the war Feall was occasionally used by the air ambulance, but a grass strip at Totronald was now the main landing ground and it was aligned on quite a different bearing from Feall. The older strip was chosen in March 1968 when Totronald was thought to be a 'no go'. The pilot, Ken Foster, takes up the story:

> After a practise approach and go-around Feall looked okay, so I set up the landing into the west wind. The Islander's normal approach speed was 65 knots and landing speed was 55 knots. Having arrived over the runway end and reduced to landing speed, my ground speed was zero. So, on touchdown I simply stood on the brakes to prevent the aircraft being blown backwards, applied the parking brake and shut down the engines. Whilst holding the flying controls central, I called through my opened window to the airstrip attendant to park his tractor close in front of the Islander to provide some degree of windbreak.
>
> With my safe arrival, the patient was brought to the aircraft and, after a struggle holding the rear door open whilst the stretcher was loaded, we soon had the aircraft tight and ready to depart. I started the engines and completed the power and pre-take off checks. With the patient and the nurse strapped in, I indicated to the attendant to drive his tractor away. The full force of the wind registered on my airspeed indicator as 55 knots, which was the take-off airspeed. I applied full power, released the wheel brakes, eased back on the elevators and the aircraft lifted off. Climbing at 65 knots I had no forward ground speed to clear the hills either side, so I had to climb to 500 feet before being safe to turn and head for Glasgow.

Despite this choice of strips, crosswinds could still pose a problem. In February 1957 a de Havilland Heron (G-ANXA) out on a training flight slithered towards a ditch on landing at Totronald. It suffered moderate damage on the starboard side but there were no crew injuries. After an inspection it was decided to partially dismantle it and ship it back to the mainland. Four old 'Fergies' – the ubiquitous grey Ferguson tractors – were called on to tow it to Breacacha beach for removal on the landing craft *Augusta*. It was repaired by the manufacturers at Hatfield and was then to fly on for another two decades.

The grass strip at Totronald became airport number three when it was more formally established in the late 1960s. This was one of a number proposed by the Highlands and Islands Development Board with a view to improving the air network in the region, and the work was done by army engineers under the OPMAC scheme – Operation Military Aid to the Community. The concrete slabs which mark the edges of the strip are still in place today, but not just so easy to find.

When the engineers had done their bit, the strip had to be inspected and approved by the Civil Aviation Authority since, compared with private or charter flights, scheduled air services bring a whole new dimension to airports. So, the 'men from the ministry' arrived (by boat!) to check, amongst other things, that the fire pump could efficiently spring into life when needed and produce an ample quantity of foam. This important test went something like:

> "Could we now please see the pump in operation."
>
> The starter button was pressed and …
>
> "Chug-a-chug, splutter, chug, chug, splutter!"
>
> Maybe just about enough foam for a bird bath!

The problem was quickly traced to the container of foam-producing liquid – empty! Cattle had somehow found access to it, taken a liking to it, and had downed a substantial quantity. Soon after that little glitch was attended to, Totronald got the 'okay' and in the early 1970s Loganair operated a scheduled service from Glasgow to Coll using the Britten-Norman twin-engined Islander aircraft. Now, how best to describe all the airport facilities? Well, there was the fire pump and the windsock. You may ask about a terminal building and the answer is that if it rained the crowds just took shelter in their vehicles or under the wing of the Islander. Security or Health and Safety? Neither, as this was all back in the 'good old days'. When the plane's arrival was imminent, a Land Rover or tractor would be driven along the strip and a check made to see if any sheep or cattle were in the vicinity and likely to stray into the danger zone. Then, when the plane came into sight, the fire pump would be started up – just in case – and similarly on departure.

After the cessation of the scheduled service into Totronald, a sloping grass strip at Ballard was established, running parallel to the road between Uig and Arileod. As well as its use by the air ambulance, there were some private/charter flights and two of these resulted in Air Accident Reports. In 1989 a single-engined Cessna was moving quite slowly near the end of its landing run when the nosewheel stuck into soft ground and collapsed. The aircraft flipped right over onto its back but the pilot, the only occupant, was unhurt. The Cessna was later dismantled and removed from the island, to be used for spares. Then, about a year later, a single-engined Piper with four occupants on board was on a take-off run towards Arileod – the *up*-slope direction – when the undercarriage caught the fence at the end of the strip. The plane then banked to the left and ended up nose-down in an adjacent field. Only the pilot sustained any injury, a minor one, and the four were able to exit through the main door. In both cases there was fortunately no fire.

Moving on swiftly to the current airfield, the last of five. In 2005, as part of a local authority initiative, finance was agreed for improvements to the airfield at Connel near Oban, and for the setting up of new airstrips on Coll and Colonsay. The thinking was that youngsters from these islands who attended Oban High School would be able to spend much more of the weekend back home by flights than what could be achieved by the ferry timetable. And the ticket price per pupil – just £1. Spare capacity was to be available to the public and, on some flights, Coll and Tiree would be linked by air. So began the construction of the first tarmac strip on the island, starting from near the bottom end of the old Ballard grass strip. It runs at quite a different bearing to the latter and the early private fliers, keen to add Coll to their pilot log books, landed and scratched their heads: "Eh? Has the prevailing wind direction suddenly swung through ninety degrees?"

The early arrivals also noted that it is not near *'civilisation'*, that mobile phone reception is virtually zero (pre-arranged transport is therefore useful), and that carrying a folding bicycle in the aircraft is a proven way to get to the village for lunch.

The completion of the runway had a very unfortunate side effect. The five miles of passable single-track road from Arinagour became virtually impassable after being pounded by heavy trucks bringing the thousands of tons of material from the new pier. In the late 1700s this was Coll's newest highway, and intended to be '… capable of a wheel-carriage …' but, considering much of it lies across an area of peat bog, it was never likely to cope well with countless 35-ton lorry loads. The road featured often in the press of 2006, with headlines such as:

> Council must cough up cash for Coll road
>
> Coll's 'repaired' road is worse than ever
>
> Island runways too short claims air experts

Hey! Where did that third headline come from? Are the lives of passengers to be put at risk? Not at all, but read on.

Eventually, in 2008, 'Coll International' was licensed for use and on Monday 16th June the first scheduled flight for over thirty years touched down. It was the return of the faithful Islander, the same type of aircraft that had been seen at Totronald in the 1970s. The island, its new airport and the scholar flights were all to feature in the evening's TV news – the BBC had the foresight to have a camera man and reporter on board for the inaugural event. So, there is now also a smooth touchdown for the air ambulance? Well, no. The fixed-wing air ambulance aircraft are no longer the Islanders and the replacements just happen to need a few more yards of tarmac. But, that is not really an issue because there are no runway lights which would aid a night-time flight. Even in daylight it is usually the helicopter that comes out to Coll, and for it there is still a suitable patch of ground at the 'top' end of the old Ballard strip, with its own windsock and ground lighting.

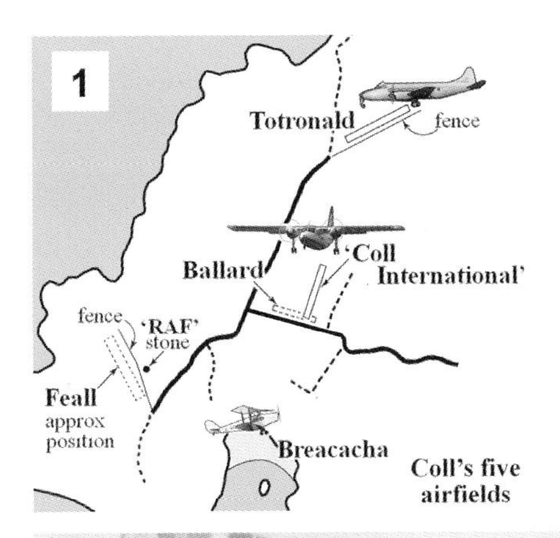

B.E.A. 'PLANE DAMAGED

Wheel Collapse on Island Landing

A de Havilland Heron aircraft of British European Airways was damaged yesterday while landing on the Island of Coll in the course of a familiarisation flight.

1. The location of Coll's five airfields. (Map: E. McGee)

2. 1933 – A de Havilland Fox Moth is being refuelled on Breacacha sands. This is the first aircraft to touch down on Coll. (Photo: Stewarts of Breacacha)

3. 1936 – Coll's first air ambulance flight. A Spartan Cruiser Mk 2 on Breacacha sands, with Captain J A Hankins & Dorothy Stewart. (Photo: Stewarts of Breacacha)

4. 1957 – This Heron suffered moderate damage but there were no crew injuries. It was returned to the manufacturers for repairs. (Photo: Stewarts of Breacacha)

5. 1970s – A Loganair Islander landing at Totronald. In the foreground is the fire pump and its two-man crew. Not a very busy day at the airport – just the photographer and one spectator. (Photo: E. McGee)

6. 2008 – The inaugural flight at 'Coll International', and carrying a BBC camera man and a reporter. (Photo: A. Sproat)

NATS (National Air Traffic Services) states that Coll now had a 500-metre asphalt strip with runway designation 02/20. NATS offers some additional advice:

> Direction and distance from city: 5 nm [nautical miles] WSW of Arinagour. [Arinagour a *city*?]
>
> Warnings: Concentrations of Greylag Geese on and around the aerodrome throughout the year.
>
> Capability for removal of disabled aircraft: Limited.
>
> Transportation: Taxi by arrangement.

Now, finally, with the hop from Tiree to Coll appearing on a timetable as a fifteen minute flight and over a distance of about eleven miles, some records need to be checked. In the Orkney Islands, Westray to Papa Westray is recognised as the world's shortest scheduled hop at two minutes – very occasionally taking less than one minute – and the distance between these airports is shorter than the runways at London's Heathrow. Coll may need to be content with a second or third place. But, if you 'lift' the perimeter fence from Heathrow and drop it on the West End it will nicely surround all five airfields. That surely is an aviation record?

Chapter 7

Kelp? Help!

Kelp?

The word initially meant the ash produced from burning seaweed, but later it came to refer also to the seaweed itself. The ash was used in the manufacture of soap and glass. This was an ideal industry for the Highlands and Islands of Scotland: the seaweed was self-renewing, the yield was dependable, virtually no capital or equipment was needed, and it could be run by unskilled labour. The seaweed was cut, pulled up onto the shore and then dried and burned in a small coffer of turf or stone. The industry would be very obvious to travellers, such as those sailing along the Sound of Mull, by columns of dull white smoke rising up from the shore, coupled with a strong and rather unpleasant smell.

The industry started on Coll about 1755 and perhaps earlier on some other islands. By the time of Johnson and Boswell's visit in 1773, Coll was shipping out about 55 tons of kelp each year. This figure later rose to a peak of 150 tons employing 140 adults, but by the mid-1830s the manufacture had almost completely ceased on the island.

The end product was shipped mainly to Merseyside where there was both a large soap manufacturing industry and a textile industry which used soap in the finishing processes. London also had soap industry but its raw material was barilla, rather than kelp, and it came from Spain, Sicily and the Canary Islands. Smacking of modern-day protectionism, the duty on barilla was fixed high enough to allow kelp to be sold at a competitive price. The profits from kelp were exceptionally high, especially during the Napoleonic Wars when the shipments of Spanish barilla were interrupted.

Help!

The cry of 'Help!' was raised in 1822. This was a significant time for the industry because the Westminster Parliament decided to reduce the duty on imported barilla by more than a half. A few years later the duty was removed completely. The reduction did not go through without vociferous representations made against it by Members of Parliament and by the Merseyside soap industry. Politicians are sometimes justifiably accused of looking for a good day to bury bad news and this old 1822 extract from Westminster may strike a chord:

> This bill, so injurious, has been brought forward in the last week of the session, and hurried through with that precipitancy which its very objectionable nature seemed to demand … No opportunity was given to those interested in the manufacture of kelp, to whom it was of vital importance to oppose it by representing their case to this house; for, in fact, this bill, so destructive, would be in operation against them … fifty thousand individuals of all classes, who were about to be reduced by this bill to beggary sad ruin …

Thousands of people were indeed reduced to poverty as a result of the bill, but there is an interesting postscript to the 1822 situation. Nearly two hundred years later, there is a Scottish soap manufacturing industry which is using the same kelp and with advertising claims for their products such as 'Using this soap will leave you feeling totally at one with the world' and 'Those who grow up near the water's edge appreciate the richness found in sea kelp'.

Chapter 8

Nights on the Nevada

BEFORE we 'go aboard' the celebrated *Nevada* we will first have a look back at lesser-known maritime incidents around the coasts of Coll. The events don't tell of wreckers and false lights. Indeed, the Rev Dr John Walker, writing in the 1700s about the islanders' need of timber, says:

> They have little but what they obtain from Shipwrecks, and with this indeed they are but too well supplied. The unfortunate Sufferers are sure of being treated with the greatest Honour and Humanity by the Inhabitants, but when the thing happens, the timber of the ship becomes a very convenient Windfall.

Most instances of grounding on the island's shores and rocks resulted from terrible weather, from gales or even hurricane-force winds and the occasional fog. Some tell of amazing rescues, by the island's life-saving corps (later the 'coastguard'), by the RNLI (the Royal National Lifeboat Institution, a volunteer service), or by the heroic act of a stricken vessel's crew member. They may tell of the sad loss of some or all of the crew. Two tragic tales are of local folk, including children, and there are times when we find island houses becoming temporary homes to the rescued.

The cause of many shipwrecks are three treacherous rocky patches, the first two lying in wait below the surface at high tide – Roan Bogha at the outer end of shoals south from Crossapol Bay, the Chieftain Rock at the mouth of Loch Eatharna and, thirdly, the notorious Cairns. The three individual rocks of the Cairns were known in the past by the islanders as An Càrn Mòr, An Càrn Beag and An Cuilean, and in 1716 Martin described them as: 'remarkable for their fatality to seafaring men, of which there are several late instances'. Now, a rather quick run through some dates and names – the full stories would fill a book by themselves!

> 1748: The *Friendship*
> 1786: A boat conveying two Members of Parliament ran onto a rock but got off safely
> 1798: HMS *Caesar* – this was a near miss and the ship was guided safely to Tobermory by an islander
> 1801: The *Mary*, of Maryport
> 1803: The *Countess of Chatham*
> 1812–September: 'On Monday the 17th ultimo, five children, having gone into a small boat at the island of Coll, they unloosened the rope by which it was fastened to the shore, and, being unable to manage it, they drifted, when they were all drowned, as the boat was got afterwards keel up.'
> 1821: The *Guadaloupe* – The factor to McLean of Coll got word to her owners that some of the cargo of rum had been salvaged:
>
> > Gallanach, Isle of Coll, 3d Feb. 1821
> >
> > Sir – I am sorry to inform you that the brig Guadaloupe, which I am informed is your property, was totally

wrecked on the west side of this Island, about five o'clock this morning. The mate, second-mate, carpenter, and one of the crew saved; the rest of the crew lost, together with an Officer belonging to the 92d Regt. or Gordon Highlanders, as also a Lady and three children, passengers. I am just now returned from looking after the cargo of which there are 15 puncheons rum and about 30 bags cotton saved; the latter damaged. This night is so boisterous and the shore so very bad, that I am doubtful everything on board will be dashed to pieces; however, all that can possibly be saved shall be taken care of till I hear from you.

1836–May: 'MELANCHOLY CATASTROPHE – On Monday the 2d current a small boat set sail from the Island of Coll for Eilean Mor, a small island adjacent, with four women, two men, and a boy, when, melancholy to relate, on returning home, the merciless vortex swallowed up the boat in a twinkling, and

The *Nevada II* (5,693 tons) aground and lying over to port at the Rubha Mòr headland, near Struan Bay. The inset shows her in better days. (The copy of the photo is courtesy of J. Fraser)

1. The Chieftain Rock buoy and, beyond it, waves washing over the rock itself. Inset shows the *Pole Star* servicing the buoy. (Photos: E. McGee)

2. At centre is the Sùil Ghorm rock and its light. In the distance are the hills of Rum. (Photo: A. McGee)

The Times January 29, 1890

A telegram from Tobermory yesterday stated that the Norwegian barque Harmonie, from Liverpool to Norway, in ballast, went ashore on Coll Island on January 26, and was dismasted. The steward was drowned; the remainder of the crew were saved.

3. The timber remains of the Norwegian barque *Harmonie* which was driven ashore at Gortan in 1890. (Photo: E. McGee)

4. 1920 – Within sight of the middle pier, this is the sad end for the *Loch Iorsa*, built in 1876 by Barclay at Ardrossan, Ayrshire. Her cargo of coal (for Coll) is being transhipped. (Photo: R. Sturgeon)

5. 1961 – Preparing to salvage the *SSAFA*. (Photo: Kennedy)

6. 1964 – The *Kaarina* aground, with the Coastguard keeping watch. (Photo: Courtesy of A. Sproat)

every soul perished, save the two men, who are very athletic, and saved themselves by swimming. This calamitous stroke of Providence has made widowers, motherless children, and orphans.'

1846: The *Eliza Moore*
1850: The *Mandane* – some of her salvaged cargo became the subject of court cases
1860: The *Francis Yates*
1861: The *Chieftain*
1864: The *Defiance*
1864: The Commissioners of Northern Lighthouses arranged for the Roan Bogha rock and the Chieftain Rock to be marked by buoys
1868: The *Michael John*
1868: The *Flora MacDonald*
1871: The *Seraphina* – re-floated
1873: The *Richard Thomson*
1873: The *Sultan*
1880: The *Saint Clair*
1880: The *Elina Cordano*
1884: The *Brickley*
1889: David Logie writes of how his companion, an ex-magistrate, spoke of a steamer being driven onto rocks during a recent severe storm. There was a young girl at the helm of the boat which came out from the island to bring the passengers safely ashore. He regarded her as a 'second Grace Darling.' The identity of this Grace is not known but speculation is that she came from Port-na-Luing
1890: The *Harmonie*
1895: The *Nessmore*
1907: The *Faraday*
1909: To mark the Cairns, a small light was constructed on Sùil Ghorm, a rocky islet off the north end of Coll – the Cairns themselves are just over half a mile further away to the north east. In comparison with other rock lights – namely the Bell Rock, Skerryvore and Dhu Heartach – Sùil Ghorm was a relatively small and easy task. However, the construction was not without its problems – huge rats! The addition of a fog gun in the winter of 1935–36 was also a challenge, as press accounts of the time tell:

> HESPERUS REACHES LONELY ROCK
>
> The lighthouse steamer *Hesperus*, after three attempts, has succeeded in landing material for the beacon on lonely Sùil Ghorm Rock. Two thousand bags of sand and gravel and two hundred of cement were transhipped to the rock in the small boat and then slung one by one up the sheer side of the 70-foot high rock. The previous attempts were abandoned owing to stormy weather. The workmen are marooned on the rock, two miles north of Coll, and are living in a small hut. It is expected the work of building the fog signal will take three months.
>
> BEACON-BUILDERS RESCUED
>
> The story of the ordeal of four men marooned on the lonely Atlantic rock for over a week by fierce storms was related at Oban last night when they were landed by the lighthouse steamer *Hesperus*. They were taken off yesterday at noon after surviving a two-day gale which threatened to sweep hut and men into the raging sea. Three weeks ago they were landed on the Sùil Ghorm Rock, two miles north of the island of Coll, to build a fog signal.

1914: The *Generalconsul Elissejeff*. With a south-east gale blowing and in pitch darkness, the Chieftain Rock buoy was mistaken for the Sùil Ghorm light, and soon the vessel was on the rocks. The lighting of a tar barrel to act as a flare let the crew see that they were very close to a rugged shore. As if things could not get worse, the fore part of the ship then caught fire from the flare, but by this time the crew had managed to get ashore with only slight injuries. They sheltered as best they could until daybreak and then they found quarters at Arinagour, from where all fourteen of them were later taken on board the MacBrayne's steamer *Dirk*. The cargo began to float about near the vessel, and local boats came out to 'assist'. It was reported in the press: 'the local receiver of wrecks in Coll will have an arduous time in superintending the collection of the floating portion of the cargo'.

1917: The *Hurlford*

1920: The smack *Loch Iorsa* with a cargo of coal – for Coll!

1925: The *Emildor*

1925: The *Arnold*

1927: The *Jan Volder*

1928: The *Saint Brandon*

1930: MacBrayne's *Cygnet* scraped the Cairns but managed back to Oban with only superficial damage

1940: The *Nydalen*

1942: The *Nevada II*

1951: The *Tapti*

1953: The *Richard Crofts*

1953: The *Angela*

1961: The Fleetwood trawler *SSAFA* (Soldiers, Sailors, Airmen and Families Association) ran aground near Friesland during a January gale, but with the help of the island's life-saving team all the crew were saved. Someone soon had a 'beady eye' on the wheelhouse which, with its removal by some oxy-acetylene burning, had the prospect of being turned into a fine hen-house. However, about three months later she was salvaged and returned to fishing, with some very successful catches. As for the hen-house – no luck! So, maybe no cluck either.

....

Now for the *Nevada* or, more properly, the *Nevada II*.

She was a 5,693-ton cargo ship launched from a German shipyard in 1915, initially the *Rovuma* but soon renamed the *Nevada II*, and she sailed for two decades with a French company. We pick up her story in July of 1942 when she was en route to Oban to join a convoy.

The Sunday started with pleasantly warm weather, but towards evening the temperature dropped as an ever-thickening fog began to move in from the Atlantic. Then the sound of a ship's siren was heard from Coll's East End. Following the direction of the siren blasts a few islanders were soon on the scene and they found the *Nevada* hard aground on rocks at the Rubha Mòr headland. It transpired that the crew had been listening for the foghorn on Sùil Ghorm, but it had been silenced for the duration of the war.

By the Monday, word of the *Nevada* had spread throughout the island, and beyond it, and quite a crowd gathered at Rubha Mòr. They cast their eyes on upper decks loaded with army vehicles and some quite splendid naval launches. Also visible up on deck back then was the ship's wartime 4-inch gun. Fifty years later, with much hard physical effort and the cooperation of many folk, this weapon was brought up from the depths and it now sits prominently by the road-side not far from the new pier.

Now, what lay hidden on her lower decks and in her holds? The quieter weather of the Sunday was being replaced by wind and rain, and the ship was being subjected to an increasing Atlantic swell. The crew thought it wise to leave the ship and they came ashore by one of her lifeboats. The islanders also thought it was a sensible move! By the time surveyors arrived on the Wednesday mailboat the sea had broken the *Nevada*'s back and the crew had little choice but to leave for the mainland.

Then the fun began! The authorised salvage work also began and the more questionable activities usually had to be carried out at night. A monkey bridge was set up to span the short distance between ship and shore – useful to the salvage workers, equally useful to the islanders! The vehicle access to the Rubha Mòr headland was improved with a short stretch of rough roadway and an aerial cable-way was rigged up to allow for the transfer of heavy material to the shore. The launches were soon in the water and off under tow to Tobermory. Some of the vehicles were also salvaged and ended up temporarily in the village where they became full-sized 'toys' to the youngsters.

On some days, word might reach the village along the lines of: "'Donnie' out at Bousd was telling me that the officials will be keeping a close eye on the ship tonight. Better pass the word around." But the more curious lads in the village might decide that, since it was a pleasant autumn evening, the few miles walk out to the ship would do them no harm and they could see what progress the salvage boys had made that day. On arrival, they would find no sign of officialdom and, venturing quietly aboard, they would stumble across 'Donnie' who had the run of the ship all to himself! 'Donnie' would have found that the cargo was very varied, although some items were to be better remembered than others:

Cigarettes: There were millions of them, with brands such as Woodbine, Players, and Gold Flake, to name but a few. A very timely arrival – the island had just run out of them!

Shoes: There was a large crate of them and 'Cinderella' fittings began until someone realised it was a case of one size fits all. Even worse, there was not a single *pair* of shoes – the crate for the other foot was never found.

Cloth: There was bale upon bale of a rather repetitive pattern but it was nevertheless very suitable for curtains, cushion covers, and the like. Childhood innocence came to the fore when a customs official exchanged some pleasantries with a mother who was pushing a pram through the village, the type of pram that had a handy storage compartment accessed by a hinged flap just below the child.

"Good morning Mrs Mac–, and how is your little one today?"

The 'little one' is wagging a finger in the general direction of the hidey hole and demonstrating one of his first Gaelic words:

"Seall, seall!" ("Look, look!")

Some cloth found its way to Oban, and onwards to Glasgow where it is known to have been used at least for nightdresses and curtains. One Collach visiting the city and planning to call on a relative knew that the address was a flat somewhere on Dumbarton Road. The realisation quickly dawned that this was a road of some considerable length – miles! Nothing daunted, the Collach began walking and in due course – maybe at Partick, the Gaeldom of Glasgow – curtains of the rather unique 'Nevada print' pattern were spotted in some windows.

Alcohol: There was not the quantity that was found on the better-known *Politician* of *Whisky Galore* fame, but one islander clearly knew where to look and after a lengthy passage of time he told his story.

"No, she had no big supply of whisky, but I did find some bottles of port, sherry and the like. I think they were for the ship's officers."

"So, how did you manage to get them ashore without being caught?"

"Well Ewen, you know how these ships have quite high sills at their doorways, perhaps as much as nine to twelve inches. And the *Nevada* was lying over at quite an angle. So, she had pools of water near many of the doorways and I found a dark corner where the water was also quite dirty. I put the bottles down lengthwise in the water, hard up against the bulkhead, and trusted that everyone would be stepping right over them between the compartment and the passageway. Then I just waited until things had quietened down and it was safe to go back on board and retrieve them."

Money: The ship's bill of lading listed ten cases of notes consigned to the Bank of British West Africa in Sierra Leone, with a total value of £75,000, and in the autumn of 1942 the financial institutions were advised in a circular that these notes were no longer legal tender. The winter of 1942/43 was wild, with severe gales hitting Coll and bringing further damage to the ship, but it was something other than a gale that buckled the door of her strongroom and allowed some notes of West African currency to be blown onto the shore. However, there was no great furore about this discovery and the salvage work continued. The war ended and island life returned to some normality, including the routine of peat cutting now that the coal in the *Nevada*'s bunkers had been exhausted.

The money story remained something of a mystery for eighteen years until a salvage operator from London, who probably thought that enough time had gone by for it to be safe, walked into a Zurich money exchange office with a quantity of West African notes. Soon a bank in London became involved, and one of their currency note dealers was rather surprised when Zurich offered him a second batch of the notes, and this time a very large amount of them. Out came the file of old circulars and he checked off the serial numbers of some notes he had already purchased and, well, the game was up! The court case that followed the inevitable arrest explained away almost £20,000 – that leaves £55,000 still to be accounted for.

The case was held in the High Court in Edinburgh, with Lord Cameron presiding and, at times, seeming to quite enjoy the event.

"Dark Horse" of the election, Glasgow himself, Jack Hou who is fighting

When the laughter had subsided he went on to tell the Court that, on his return from leave in 1943, he saw currency notes in the ship. There were also notes on the beach.

He identified the notes, from samples shown to him in court, as having been West African currency notes and admitted he had kept some.

Asked what he did with the notes, he replied – "I gave them to the children to play with."

SALVAGE MAN GETS NINE MONTHS

By a majority verdict, a jury at the High Court in Edinburgh yesterday found a ship salvage man Guilty of stealing £19,749 in West African notes from the wreck of the Nevada II, which went ashore on the Isle of Coll

Board notes. On one occasion brought him a suitcase full of the notes.

The equivalent of about £19,000 had been paid to in Swiss francs before a message received in Zurich from London indicated that the notes concerned were no longer legal tender, he added. Mr. Arnold said that he then got in touch with the police.

The trial was adjourned until tomorrow.

Macmillan said that in face of the sive nuclear testing programmes d out by the Russians since 1961 we onfined ourselves to the minimum

Mr Bremner said that ng his time on Coll he was ity receiver of wrecks and a ial constable.

On an island . . .

Mr Bremner said he had never actually met , having only once passed him on the road, but he agreed he knew who he was.

Asked how he knew, the ex-crofter remarked – "On an island like Coll we all know everyone else."

Lord Cameron – "And everything that goes on?" – Yes.

THE "money galore" case at the High Court in Edinburgh to-day provided a comic touch worthy of another celebrated Hebridean shipwreck story.

20S. NOTES BLOWING ABOUT ISLE

WRECK THEFT CHARGE

FROM OUR CORRESPONDENT EDINBURGH

The day on which West African bank notes were found blowing about the tin Island of Coll in the Hebrides was described by Mr. James MacKinnon, aged 62, a farmer on the island, at the High Court in Edinburgh today.

McCulloch Cunningham, Argyll Constabulary, spoke of having taken possession of pass-port when he charged him in his home in London. The passport bore stamps relative to Zurich on February 2 and 6, 1960, and Belgium on February 5, 1960.

"Salvage official told me money was of no value"

"I FOUND TWO TIN CASES OF NOTES ON NEVADA"

of 10s notes, but he was unable to recollect if their total value was £700.

In answer to Mr Kissen Mackinnon said he handed the notes over to the Receiver of Wrecks.

Mr Kissen – Did any islanders go aboard the ship? – I don't know.

Mr Kissen – They went over your land. Did they go in the direction of the Nevada II? – Yes.

Mr Kissen – This was at night? – Yes.

he National Farmers' Union, told a meeting of the Farmers' Clubs in London esterday.

The dismantling of Britain's

A number of press cuttings from 1962, most of them relating directly to the *Nevada* trial in the High Court, Edinburgh. (Composite arrangement: E. McGee)

Mr Kissen, counsel for the accused, questioned the special constable who was on the island at the time of the grounding. The constable said that he had never actually met the accused, but agreed he knew who he was.

> Mr Kissen: "*How* did you know?"
> "On an island like Coll we all know everyone else."
> Lord Cameron: "And everything that goes on?"
> "Yes."

Another witness, an island farmer, told how he found bundles of notes on the shore but was unable to remember their total value. He said that he had handed the notes over to the Receiver of Wrecks.

> Mr Kissen: "Did any islanders go aboard the ship?"
> "I don't know."
> Mr Kissen: "They went over your land. Did they go in the direction of the *Nevada II*?"
> "Yes."
> Mr Kissen: "This was at night?"
> "Yes."

And just what evidence will you find on Coll today? Visitors mostly arrive at the island's ferry terminal and about 200 yards up the road on the right-hand side they will find the *Nevada*'s gun, pointing towards Mull. A few miles away at the Rubha Mòr headland can be seen the short stretch of roadway. Over a low ridge from the end of the rough road are the concrete blocks that held the aerial cableway and this is just the spot to look down wistfully on the salty grave of the *Nevada*. Nothing is now visible above the surface, even on a low spring tide. But will anyone ever come across any of the missing £55,000?

Tourist Tip:

Use of any wartime West African currency notes is probably best limited to a game of Monopoly.

Chapter 9

A Fairy Tale ... and a Ferry Tale

ONCE upon a time … and we don't know what time is meant but it was later, in 1906, when the Rev Dugald MacEchern wrote down the tale he had heard regarding a location near Gallanach on Coll:

> The Fairy Rings. There are four rings, two large and two small ones. Each ring is a band of grass darker than the rest of the grass, the band being about a foot broad and running round in a circle of about eight yards diameter in the case of the large rings, and of six feet diameter in the case of the smaller. The grass is neither longer nor shorter than the rest, the ground being all perfectly smooth, but the difference in the colour perfectly marks out the circles which almost touch one another. White mushrooms in their season grow on the rings, but neither outside them nor inside, but merely on the circumference; hence the rings are white. These are, I suppose, the fairy circles of the children's songs –
>
> *Merrily, merrily let us sing,*
> *Dancing in a Fairy Ring.*
>
> The farmer at Gallanach tells me there are similar circles on Ben Feall. He is not superstitious, but he has seen the hares scampering round the circles, and it is well known that hares have dealings with the fairy world.

And Kirsty Campbell, perhaps hearing of MacEchern's tale or hearing other similar tales from her ancestors, has in her Isle of Coll song lyrics: '… on to green Ben Feall … where the fairies danced at twilight, so the old folks used to say'.

Once upon a calm summer's day about 1960, Coll's sturdy little red wooden ferry boat (the *Coll*) manoeuvres and ties up alongside the cargo ship which is anchored out in the bay.

"What have you got for us today?" the ferryman calls up to the bridge.

"Nine and a half tons!" is the reply which floats down.

The ferryman is standing next to a framed Board of Trade certificate which he knows only too well states that the *Coll's* limit is two and a half tons … (Mmm. Nine and a half … divided by two and a half … that's four trips … but the tide's still on the flood and it's a spring tide … won't get the ferry near the pier crane for another three or four hours … need a lot of hands on the crane … could be two tides, maybe even three, for this load …)

"Well, let's see what we can do!"

The result was that all nine and a half tons were carefully loaded, with as much heavy material as possible being positioned low down between the thwarts in order to maintain good stability. The *Coll* was visibly well down to the gunwales as she came puttering back to the middle pier. Then there was the expected long wait for the tide to rise sufficiently and allow her to get close to the crane for the lengthy unloading to begin.

In the early 1960s, Coll's ferryboat, the *Coll*, approaches the middle pier with 9½ tons of cargo on board. Also on board was a framed Board of Trade certificate stating a maximum load of 2½ tons. (Photo: E. McGee 8mm cine)

Chapter 10

Collywood

Coll – a 1958 film location!

JUST after World War II some organisations got together to discuss the lack of cultural and recreational facilities in the Scottish crofting counties. The main concern was the lack of cinemas and this gave birth to the Highlands and Islands Film Guild. The object of the Guild was to bring quality films to rural communities on a non-profit-making basis by means of 16mm cinema vans, each van carrying its own electricity generator. Just for the record, the Hillswick district of the Shetland mainland was the location of the Guild's first ever film show, in April 1947.

You may wonder how it worked on Coll where, clearly, a van could not readily be brought ashore for a single evening's show – no such things then as roll-on/roll-off ferries. A few days in advance of the event a notice would appear in the shop window and, also in ample time, the 'fillum' itself would arrive on the mailboat. The electricity for the projector came from a generator in a shed at the end of the village hall. When that power supply was being troublesome a cable was run across the road to the 'genny' at the doctor's house and that extra distance did help you to hear the soundtrack better. On the big evening the cinema-goers would be seen heading for the hall, and the experienced ones would each be carrying a cushion. The curtains were drawn tightly on the windows and it was on with the show. The flickering on the screen showed the familiar old countdown: 8 … 7… 6 … etc. If there was not an 8 … 7… 6 … then probably the previous user of the film had forgotten to rewind a reel and there then would be a very early intermission.

A poster from about 1963, although not for a Coll 'fillum' show. But, just look at the prices: 3/3 for adults and 1/9 for children – about 16p and 8p in decimal currency! (Poster is courtesy of I. Goode, Theatre Film and Television Studies, University of Glasgow)

1) Both sides of the Machine slide out – operation of the left side is shown here. 2) With the interior at its full width, both side aisles – and their attached seats – can then be folded down, as seen here. There are some finishing touches to be done, e.g. turning the screen to lie across the vehicle. (Stills from a film taken on the Isle of Mull are courtesy of Regional Screen Scotland.)

At the end of the first reel of the feature 'fillum' the lights went on (or just some curtains opened?) while the reels were changed and everyone had a chat, a walkabout, a smoke – and a rub of sore posteriors by those without cushions! Sometimes there were extra intermissions when the film broke and had to be spliced, and similarly if the projectionist managed to get the reels out of sequence. By contrast to all of this, the rural parts of Scotland now have visits from the Screen Machine, an 80-seat air-conditioned mobile cinema with comfortable seating, the latest surround sound system, wheelchair facilities, etc. In about one hour after parking, it has 'unfolded' itself and is ready for business. As for the actual 'unfolding', see the photographic explanation. On 12th August 2013, the Screen Machine made its first visit to Coll and, just to record some details for the archives, there were showings of two new films – *Despicable Me 2* and *World War Z*.

The use of Coll as a movie location came in 1958 when cameras and film crew came ashore to capture some footage for the colour comedy *The Bridal Path*. This was adapted for the screen by the British Lion Film Corporation from a Nigel Tranter novel, and it starred Bill Travers. In the movie, Coll actually represents the mainland from which Bill is trying to get back to his fictional island, while he has policemen and a police dog hot on his heels. At the island's beautiful

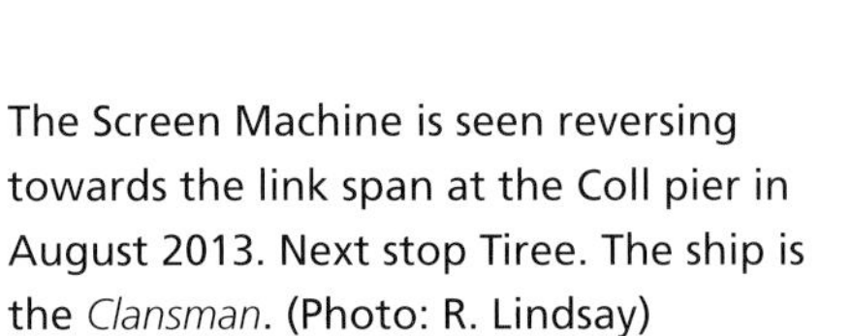

The Screen Machine is seen reversing towards the link span at the Coll pier in August 2013. Next stop Tiree. The ship is the *Clansman*. (Photo: R. Lindsay)

Left: a poster for the 1959 film – *The Bridal Path*.
Right: stills from the outdoors Sorisdale scene.
a) Bill Travers coming down to the beach at Sorisdale.
b) Bill checking the boat looks okay.
c) Bill heading up to the house to negotiate the purchase of the boat.
(Monochrome stills courtesy of STUDIOCANAL Films Limited)

North Shore a girl in a swimming costume draws Bill's attention and he follows her hopefully along the sand, only to find his path soon blocked by a menacing, hairy-chested male – one of the film crew acting as an extra. Bill turns back and is next seen coming down the hillside to Sorisdale where his eye latches on to a small boat on the beach – perhaps a way for him to leave the 'mainland'? He inspects it and turns back to a little white shore-side cottage, thinking of negotiating a price for it with the ladies who are sitting outside. For all those who knew the thatched house at Sorisdale it its heyday, it was quickly obvious that the footage of all the interior scenes belonged to a studio set!

Screen personalities say: "Don't work with animals!" The script for Sorisdale was that the police dog 'Rex' would run down the beach and bark ferociously at Bill as he pushed off the boat to row away from the 'mainland'. However, having taken a liking to Bill, the dog ran into the sea and jumped up to join him in the boat, as it did on a number of re-takes. The dog won, and the script was adjusted accordingly!

Chapter 11

Halcyon (?) Days of Travel

THE MODERN ease with which you can reach Coll from the mainland, by either a thirty-minute flight from Connel or a three-hour voyage from Oban, might be contrasted to travel in earlier years. Until the 1850s there was virtually no scheduled service to the island, and the sea conditions plus wind speed and direction were major factors in being able to reach the place at all.

A breakthrough came in 1852 when it then became possible to journey all the way from the Clyde to Coll without changing vessels, just going ashore for overnight accommodation. Based on various publications and records of that time, the journal of a fictitious traveller to Coll might well have read as follows:

> *Tuesday, 11th July, 1854.* I made my way to the Broomielaw in Glasgow for a 6 am departure on the *Cygnet*, one of David Hutcheson's small paddle steamships, although I could have left the city two hours later by train and caught up with her at Greenock. On the first part of the journey down river I noticed many ships at various stages of construction. Then there was countryside on both banks until we reached Govan and, on the opposite bank, Partick with its mills. My Lumsden Steamboat Companion Guide's description of Govan as a 'prettily situated little village with a handsome church' is very accurate. We made good progress throughout the day, with stops at places such as Greenock, Rothesay and East Tarbert, and in the evening arrived at Ardrishaig, entered the Crinan Canal and stopped for the night. I obtained accommodation at the inn.

The *Clansman* approaching Coll in December 2012, in a slightly choppy sea. She did manage to tie up and land passengers and vehicles, and that says much for the captain, the deck crew and the pier staff. (Photo: E. McGee)

> *Wednesday, 12th July, 1854.* The journey today started with the passage of the canal. It was pleasant to walk on the towpath and let the steamboat go at its own pace through the locks. I went back on board before we reached Crinan and a fellow passenger told me of an incident that I had missed. It seems that a very portly person had joined the ship at Lochgilphead and was seen standing right at the deck edge. The captain shouted to him, "Keep away from the side of the boat! Stand in the middle, or you'll

upset it." A member of the crew explained the reason for the captain's concern. The *Cygnet*'s paddles do not stick out from the sides as they do on other ships but, rather, they are tucked away and make her narrow enough to use the Canal. It also means that she is narrower down at the water where the paddles are and she is more likely to list and roll badly. After that, even I decided to stay away from the deck edge. As we left the western end of the canal and entered the open sea again I was rather apprehensive about the prospect of inclement weather. My guidebook has a nicely-worded little caveat at this point: 'The steamer's pathway is so completely landlocked that there are no high seas to be encountered, though at times, in passing the Slate Islands, the swell from the Atlantic in fresh weather may somewhat discompose unaccustomed constitutions.' Late in the afternoon we passed between the Island of Kerrera and

DIRECT STEAM COMMUNICATION
BETWEEN
GLASGOW AND LOCHMADDY (NORTH UIST),
AND BETWEEN
GLASGOW AND THE ISLANDS OF COLL AND TIREE,
unless prevented by any unforeseen occurrence.

The STEAMER DUNTROON CASTLE, CAPTAIN MACDONALD, will Sail from GLASGOW for LOCHMADDY, NORTH UIST, on Thursday the 25th March, at 2 P.M.—Train to Greenock, 4 P.M.

The Steamer CYGNET or LAPWING will Sail from GLASGOW for the ISLANDS of COLL and TIREE, on Tuesday the 23d March, at 6 A.M.—Train to Greenock at 8 A.M.

For farther information apply to the Proprietors,
DAVID HUTCHESON & CO.,
14 Jamaica Street.
Glasgow, 11th February 1852.

February 1852 – One of the earliest adverts for a direct steamship service between the Clyde and Coll/Tiree.

the mainland and came into Oban. The guidebook describes the accommodation on offer as: 'The Caledonian Hotel, a very commodious and well-conducted establishment, two or three other inns of less pretensions, and a large proportion of the inhabitants lay themselves out for the accommodation of lodgers.' I chose the Caledonian.

Thursday, 13th July, 1854. Another early start and soon we were passing Lismore and the Linnhe Loch. Before noon we were tied up at Tobermory and this really is an attractive place. The lower part of the town extends in a crescent round part of the bay and is formed of clean well-built houses and some shops. Tobermory is, of course, famous for the *Florencia* which belonged to the Armada. I remember hearing that McLean of Coll had obtained some pieces of fine foreign wood from her and had them made into chimney ornaments to adorn Breacacha. About an hour after leaving Tobermory the sea was less smooth. I found out that we were now off a headland called Caliach Point, known for its turbulent waters, but within another hour we arrived at Arinagour and came alongside a clean new pier.

H. Rider Haggard describes his Coll arrival in 1898:

> From Oban to Coll the traveller goes by steamboat, a journey of six or seven hours. After Ardnamurchan Point is left behind come ten or twelve miles of open water, which, when the swell is pressing in from the Atlantic, have been known to interfere with the digestions of the hardiest … at length, running round a point [the Meall] about which hang gannet and other diving birds we enter what is by courtesy called a harbour. I say "by courtesy," for if the wind is blowing hard, especially from the sou'-east, it is impossible for the steamer to communicate with the shore. Presently a broad-bottomed boat comes out, into which we are bundled with our luggage, some other passengers returning from the gathering at Oban, several black-faced rams, and a sheepdog.

And Haggard's departure:

> It is not always easy to escape from Coll, and in the grey dark of a winter morning many and anxious are the inquiries as to the strength and direction of the wind. "I doubt ye'll no win to her. It's blawin' hard from the sou'-east", said the old butler, 'her' being, of course, the steamer. When we arrived at the harbour there were no signs of the *Fingal*, but presently along the cable came the ominous intelligence that she had been unable to communicate with Tiree. Now we began to think that it would be our fate to stop on Coll for longer than we were expected. It is told, indeed, that people have been detained for six weeks; but this was in the old days of the sailing packet, when there was no possibility of communicating with other shores even by telegraph. As the boatmen, however, were of opinion that the steamer would put in, we followed the mails and luggage into a large flat bottomed boat and were rowed away across the harbour to the shelter of some rocks upon the further side. Presently in she came and dropped anchor, and we started towards her, pitching and tossing across the stormy water. It requires a good deal of skill to bring a boat alongside without accident in such heavy weather, and when he jumps for the vessel as she rolls towards him the passenger needs agility and decision. However, we all scrambled aboard without mishap, and steamed to Oban in pouring rain.

George Blair, purser on the steamer *Hebrides*, wrote of an incident during the First World War:

> The greatest scare we had was when we were on a passage between Tobermory and Coll. A vessel following at a distance fired a shot at us. It was presumably a blank, for she turned out to be a patrol gunboat. Of course, when our Skipper realised that the shot had been fired by her he had the *Hebrides* slowed down.
>
> "Did you not see my signal?" were the angry words from the gunboat.
>
> "No. How could I when we were both steering in the same direction and you have your flags flying fore and aft?"
>
> "Do you see my signal now?" the captain was then asked gruffly.
>
> "I do," he replied. (Apparently the signal was 'Hostile submarine in vicinity'.)
>
> We carried on to Coll and I am glad to say we had no encounter with the raiding submarine.

A traveller recollects conditions in the 1960s:

> As a child, the holiday always started just as soon as we boarded the train at Glasgow. It departed very late in the evening, maybe about 11.30 p.m. It certainly didn't go like the clappers because it always had to wait a while at Stirling where I think there was an important connection, maybe with a London to Aberdeen train.
>
> There was one occasion when a farmer joined the train at Stirling and came into our compartment. I think the livestock sales had given good prices – he had a satisfied smile and a distinctively alcoholic odour. He looked at us with interest:
>
> "You folks going as far as Oban? Oh, good! Can you make sure I get off at Dalmally?"
>
> Soon, he was sound asleep!
>
> From Stirling, the route was by Callander, Strathyre and Lochearnhead, then a slow climb up through Glen Ogle where the line hugged the contours of the hillside, and on to Crianlarich.
>
> As youngsters, we could survive a night with little sleep – there was so much to savour: the sound of the steam locomotive echoing off the hillsides … in the early light of day, the spectacle of the Pass of Brander and the unique trip-wires next to the line (still in use today) which set signals to red should a boulder dislodge itself from the slopes of Ben Cruachan and

> roll down onto the track … the rattle of milk churns being wheeled along some station platform … the sound of bagpipes from far down the train … much Gaelic chatter and laughter in an adjacent compartment … Oban! The cry of gulls, the smell of the sea, the faithful *Claymore* waiting for us … an excellent breakfast on board, with that memorable silver service … a short stop at picturesque Tobermory … up on deck the bagpipes play on, now a little more 'lubricated'… then a call to get down below to the side door, and once it is opened the red ferryboat is seen bobbing out to meet us. Coll – we have arrived again!

And today? Well, some of the 'pleasures' that accompanied the ferryboat have gone. No longer is there the routine of a large crowd meeting the ferryboat and making you feel especially welcome as you step ashore. Reasonable agility is no longer a pre-requisite for getting ashore – i.e. the ability to step between two moving vessels. Now though it may sometimes be a case of driving off a ship's vehicle ramp that is moving rather more than you would prefer – horizontally and vertically – and onto the pier's link span.

Tourist Tip:

Drivers should obey the signals of the deck crew and should not treat the ship's stern ramp as a chicane on a motor racing circuit! There is the very occasional day when perhaps only some of the traffic for Coll manages to land before a mooring rope snaps, the ramp has to be hoisted, and the ship must make her way out to sea, and then probably straight back to Oban. Better safe than sorry.

Chapter 12

Sister Jean Kennedy

A PARTICULARLY sad time for Coll was late September in 1957. A Heron air ambulance aircraft crashed on the island of Islay while trying to land in atrocious weather, with the loss of all three people on board. The nurse from Glasgow's Southern General Hospital who had volunteered in her off-duty hours was Jean Kennedy from Coll, and she had already flown on more than two hundred mercy trips.

Sister Jean Kennedy, also known as Sister Kindness, was a highly respected nurse and she was remembered in the hospital by the dedication of a lectern, and by a nursing award: the Jean Kennedy Memorial Gold Medal. The first winner of the medal described Jean as someone that the students always looked up to. Then a Heron aircraft was named *Sister Jean Kennedy*, and the name was carried forward as newer types of plane joined the air ambulance service. The Islay incident is recorded on a plaque at that island's airport and it is also recorded on a cairn close to the site of Renfrew Airport, from where the fateful flight began. The cairn is located on the corner of Sandy Road with Newmains Road, and at the end of 2013 Renfrew Community Council was reporting on plans to give the site a complete facelift. The cairn has the wording:

> This cairn is erected by the Town Council of the Royal Burgh of Renfrew as a tribute to the men and women of the Scottish Air Ambulance Service who operated from Renfrew Airport in all possible weather conditions, from 1933 until the Airport closed on 30th April 1966 and who by their courage, skill and selfless devotion to duty, drove the fear of serious illness from the islands. The plinth contains stones from the islands and other places which these gallant airmen and nurses served so faithfully.
>
> This cairn also pays homage to the memory of the following members of the service who lost their lives at Islay when answering a call for help on 28th September, 1957
>
> Captain T.M. Calderwood
> Radio Officer H. McGinlay
> Nursing Sister J. Kennedy

Before the time when the Southern General Hospital began to provide staff for the air ambulance the rural communities had to temporarily do without the services of those nurses who accompanied patients on flights to the mainland. That usually left quite a gap in health care, since small isolated places in Scotland have long found it difficult to appoint and retain the services of doctors and nurses. Coll and Tiree are no exceptions to this. The Old Statistical Account of the 1790s tells of three successful courses of inoculation on Tiree, bringing about an increase in the population. The ailment is not quoted, but very likely it was smallpox which was rife at this time. The same Account pleads for a resident doctor.

Then the New Statistical Account of 1843 for the combined Parish of Tiree and Coll tells how in the first half of the nineteenth century some young male doctors set up in practice, but found the remuneration inadequate and soon left in disgust. The difficulty

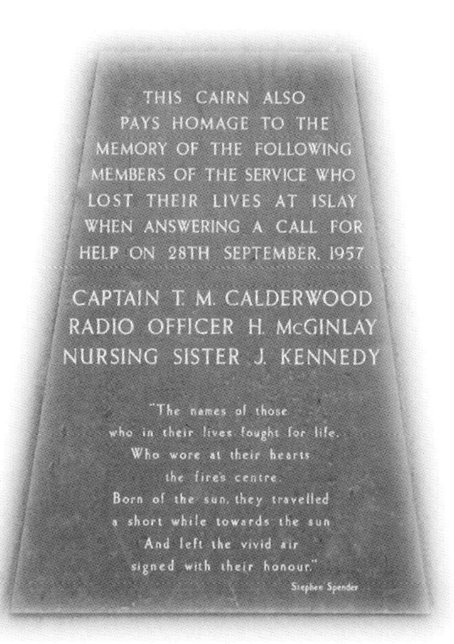

Sister Jean Kennedy (Photo: Kennedy/MacRae) and both sides of the cairn at Renfrew (Photos: E. McGee)

continued into the twentieth century, when the plea continued to be voiced for doctors and nurses to work in the Mull, Coll and Tiree area.

By the time that the situation on Coll began to improve the doctors were generally incomers to the area. However, the island was fortunate to have been served by one Collach – Robert Paterson, who was schooled first at Arnabost and later at Acha. After qualifying, he had a medical practice in Lanarkshire for many years, but the evening of his days were devoted to the patients of his native island where, as on the mainland, he was held in high esteem.

Today, Coll has a medical practice in a new purpose-built building, and it also has a modern ambulance. A benefit from the new airport and its scheduled flights is the ability for islanders to attend hospital appointments in Oban and be back home on the same day. To the same new building there is a routine visit from a mainland dentist, to perform check-ups. If any treatment is required then the patient needs to make a journey in the opposite direction. Above all, when needed, there are still the personnel of the excellent Air Ambulance Service which, as the cairn at Renfrew says: '… by their courage, skill and selfless devotion to duty, drove the fear of serious illness from the islands.' On the same cairn is an extract from a 1933 work by the poet Sir Stephen Spender (1909–1995) entitled 'The Truly Great':

> The names of those who in their lives fought for life,
> Who wore at their hearts the fire's centre.
> Born of the sun they travelled a short while towards the sun
> And left the vivid air signed with their honour.

Chapter 13

The Pulpit

> The Free Churchmen took forcible possession of the church at Arinagour, in the Isle of Coll, on Saturday afternoon. The usual method was pursued of demanding the keys from the minister, and on these being refused bursting open the church door and substituting new locks for the old ones.
>
> A cutting from the *Scotsman* newspaper of December, 1904.

IN THE autumn of 2012 it seemed as if there might soon be another change of Free Church door locks, and maybe even a change of doors – and windows – as well. Dating from 1884, the building in Arinagour was up for sale, with the possibility of it being converted for some entirely different use. The incident referred to in the 1904 press cutting stemmed from the union of the Free Church and the United Presbyterian Church to form the United Free Church. This was not welcomed in every quarter of the Free Church, and there were other parishes in Scotland where access to church premises became a contentious issue.

The beginnings of Christianity on Coll could very well be as early as 600 AD. Baithene (or Baithne), a contemporary of Columba and who sailed with him to Scotland, had a monastic settlement on Tiree. Given their proximity, there was very likely some communication between the two islands at that time.

The remains of ten old chapels have been identified on Coll, each with an adjacent burial ground. One ruin is sited in the current cemetery at Killunaig (Cill Ionnaigh/Kilfinnaig) on the East End road, and it is dated to between 1300 AD and 1500 AD. Killunaig is probably the 'Kirktoun' (or 'Churchtown') which has a 1528 reference in *The Antiquities Ecclesiastical and Territorial of the Parishes of Scotland.* The prefix 'Kil' means church and Coll had four such place-names: Kilbride, Killunaig, Kilkenneth and Kilchainie. Kilbride is still a recognised location even although the current house of that name was built in the 1880s. The earlier Kilbride steadings were nearer the coast, and a circular wall enclosed a possible burial ground even although there are no traces of gravestones or of a chapel. As for Kilkenneth and Kilchainie, these are now hardly known of but they seem to have been located in the Ballehogh to Grishipol area.

If we could travel back in time a few hundred years we would see a bell hanging in one end of the Killunaig chapel. Rumour has it that the bell was removed in the dark one night to nearby Gallanach farm and later used there to summon the farm workers home when dinner was ready.

The chapel goes back to pre-Reformation days and it was a McLean chief from Coll who, on finding himself in agreement with the doctrines of the reformed church, converted some of his tenants to presbyterianism. They were on their way to chapel when McLean,

Tourist Tip:

The top parts of the chapel walls are visible in the northern part of the cemetery. The site has been excavated, down as far as the window embrasures, and then filled in again to preserve things for more work at a later date. The depth to which the building has been covered tells of the effect of blown sand over a prolonged period.

holding a gold-headed cane, ushered them to a barn where a presbyterian clergyman was to preach. This event could have taken place on the Isle of Rum or the Isle of Mull but, wherever, it led to a saying that his religion was that of the yellow-headed stick.

As regards Christian literature, Johnson and Boswell noted in 1773 that the minister of the time, Hector MacLean, did not favour the Erse [Irish Gaelic] translation of the New Testament. It was another thirty years before the Bible in Scottish Gaelic became readily available. Writing about Hector MacLean, Boswell adds: 'He has no publick edifice for the exercise of his ministry, and can officiate to no greater number than a room can contain. This is all the opportunity of worship that is now granted to the inhabitants of the Island, some of whom must travel thither perhaps ten miles.'

It was 1802 before a good-sized church building was completed, at Clabbach, but even then many worshippers would still have had a walk of some miles each Sunday. In 1898, H. Rider Haggard wrote of the walk: 'People who grumble because they have to go half a mile to find a church door would scarcely praise the spiritual facilities of Coll, for from the Castle to Clabac is a good five miles, or an hour and a half of steady walking.'

A second big ecclesiastical change came with the Disruption of 1843, when hundreds of ministers left the Church of Scotland to form what became the Free Church of Scotland. One of these ministers was Archibald Nicol on Coll. The McLean laird of the time was seldom on the island but he had taken exception to some statements of the Free Church and refused the Coll people a site for building a separate church. He as good as copied his ancestor, McLean of the yellow-headed stick, and sent word to the people that on a certain Sunday he would present them with a minister of his choosing. On the set day he stationed himself beside the existing church and remonstrated with the islanders. Respectfully but firmly they refused to comply with his wishes and streamed past to join Mr Nicol in an open air service.

So, where could these new congregations meet for worship? In many places landowners who were loyal to the Church of Scotland were reluctant to provide a piece of ground for Free Church adherents to put up a building. Some innovative solutions arose, such as having a structure situated on the foreshore between the high and low water marks – not Crown land in Scotland – or, in the case of Loch Sunart, having a 700-seat floating church built on Clydeside and towed to the desired site. For Coll, the problem was not quickly resolved and the situation was noted at the May 1860 Assembly of the Free Church, when it was reported: 'They have no place of worship save in cottages or in the open air. The minister cannot procure any lodging except in a hovel, from the damp and cold of which he is obliged to protect himself by hot-water bottles.' However, a few years later, Grishipol farmhouse was built as the first Free Church manse and what is now an adjoining barn at the roadside was the church itself.

Both Coll and neighbouring Tiree were to experience Christian revivals some years before the better known ones on the Isle of Lewis and in Wales. The most stirring time on Tiree was the autumn of 1874 when there was a period of nightly meetings. A minister wrote of the events to a friend and told how the Balemartine church was full by 5 pm when the service was not due to start until 7 pm, and these meetings were on busy harvest days. Help was clearly needed and Alexander Fraser, Coll's Free Church minister, went across for a few weeks to assist. Then, a few years later:

> *Edinburgh Evening News* – Friday 14 March 1879
>
> RELIGIOUS MOVEMENT IN THE ISLAND OF COLL
>
> The people of the Island of Coll have for several weeks manifested such deep and increasing interest in attending divine services both on week days and on Sundays, that the

1. Looking westwards in 2008 at the Killunaig chapel ruins, most of the height of the walls being hidden below ground level – such is the effect of hundreds of years of blown sand. Above the ground are the walls which surround the cemetery. (Photo: E. McGee)

2. A 1786 engraving by Thomas Rowlandson showing a seated Johnson in discussion with the minister, Hector MacLean, who has his back to the fire. Boswell listens on with interest. "We called by the way on Mr Hector MacLean, the Minister of Col ... Mr MacLean has the reputation of great learning: he is seventy-seven years old, but not infirm, with a look of venerable dignity, excelling what I remember in any other man."

3. The attractive Struan cottage at the roadside, in 2008. The Mission House is the small part on the far right, with the lighter grey corrugated roof. (Photo: E. McGee)

4. 2007 – The interior of the Church of Scotland in Arinagour. (Photo: E. McGee)

> Rev Mr Fraser, Free Church minister, feels it his duty to apply for help to carry on the work. By the appointment of the Free Church Committee for the Highlands and Islands, the Rev Mr McPherson, Cawder, and the Rev Mr Cameron, Govan, have for the last fortnight given their services. In the daytime and in the evenings evangelistic meetings were held in different townships in the island. These meetings were crowded, and pervaded with great solemnity and deep impression, so much so that strong stalwart men were seen to shed tears copiously. Last Sunday the Sacrament of the Lord's Supper was dispensed, when a congregation that overcrowded the church, sat from half-past eleven till four o'clock. The pastor of this congregation has this year added a larger number to his communion roll than he has done for the last 20 years put together.

On Coll, the Free Church also used a small mission house attached to the end of the roadside cottage at Struan. When revival hit Coll in the late 1870s this tiny church was packed full, with an overflow crowd outside. In the early 1900s there were further revivals but, despite these, the church was to experience a steady reduction in the numbers attending worship just as the island population was also on the decline. Most visitors arrive by sea and even from quite a distance they may note the current Church of Scotland sitting prominently above the village. This was built in 1907 and stemmed largely from the efforts of the Rev Dugald MacEchern. We may finish this chapter on a brighter note – it is acceptable now to have preachers of different Christian persuasions in its pulpit, just maybe not two at the same time.

Chapter 14

Blackboard, Chalk and Sand

April 29, 1725: The General Meeting settled one school in the Isle of Coll with 100 merks of Salary.

THE ABOVE is thought to be the earliest account of a school on Coll and it is from the records of the Society in Scotland for Propagating Christian Knowledge (SSPCK). The same account continues:

> August 10: Schoolmaster commifsion to Mr James Stewart with Salary commencing from Lambas Last.[1]
>
> August 11: 12 Dozen syllabicating catechisms, 20 quires of paper, 1 musick book & 1 Arithmetick book sent with Mr James Stewart master.
>
> Jan 1726: Books, Thirty six Bibles, Thirty New Testaments, Twenty confefsions of faith, Ten Vincents Catechisms[2], Ten Guthrie's trial[3], three Arithmetick Books, three musick books, eight dozen of catechisms, six dozen of proverbs, half a rheam of paper sent by Mr Lauchlan Mclean.

1. Probably Lammas Day, in August, one of the four terms days in Scotland – Candlemas, Whitsunday, Lammas Day, and Martinmas – the term days for the beginning and ending of employment of servants.
2. The Westminster Shorter Catechism was explained from Scripture in 1674 by a Thomas Vincent.
3. Probably a reference to a small publication called *Guthrie's Trial of a Saving Interest in Christ*, written by a William Guthrie who was ordained as a minister in 1644.

The location of this early school is not known and, while well supported, does not appear to have lasted for more than about a year. Then, in 1794, a more permanent SSPCK school was established at Grimsary, and at one point it had no fewer than 105 pupils attending. A distinguished pupil of this school was Lachlan McLean (Lachlan na Gaidhlig, 1798–1848) from Arnabost. By 1824 the SSPCK had a school a mile or so away at Clabbach, maybe a relocation from Grimsary, and a visiting inspector reported that there were thirty-five scholars, but rising to fifty in the winter when there was less demand for extra hands around the croft.

Some other organisations also established schools on the island during the 1800s. The Gaelic Schools Society set up its first school on Coll at the Braes of Toraston in 1813 and the shell of the building still stands in that almost empty township. A year after its opening it had a roll of between forty to sixty pupils. Other sites of the Gaelic Schools in Coll were at Ardnish, Kilbride, Acha, Caolas, Leachdruadh, Ceann a Bhaigh and Bousd. The school buildings were often little more than humble shelters but the teachers gave devoted service. David Fowler, a teacher at Bousd, led his pupils down to the beach and used the firm sand for writing practice. The Church of Scotland set up many schools (known as General Assembly Schools), eventually having about 200 throughout Scotland with one of these being in Arinagour, and the Free Church Ladies' Association established a school in the roadside house at Struan.

The island's main proprietor, John Lorne Stewart, arranged for a new school to be built at Acha in 1863. The school and schoolhouse exist today, but much modified for use solely as a dwelling house. Later, Stewart added a school at Arnabost, the conspicuous roofless building close to the 'T' junction. One pupil tells of his school-day walk to Acha:

> Ewen, when you were going to school in Glasgow I'm sure you stopped some days at the sweetie shop and spent a bit of pocket money – and didn't do your teeth much good. Well, Coll never had a sweetie shop in the West End, but I could stop at the Acha corn mill. The taste of freshly ground corn was quite a treat and maybe just as nice as your sweeties!

The Education Act of 1872 resulted in the transfer of the schools at Acha and Arnabost to the School Board and the early 1890s saw the building of new Board schools at Arinagour (the tall building, now converted to two storeys, standing prominently at the top of the hill) and at Cornaig. Under the Act, it became law for every child to receive basic schooling between the ages of five and twelve. This resulted in problems for a number of remote communities throughout Scotland

Acha – part of the school is shown on the left and the adjoining schoolhouse is on the right. The whole building has since been substantially altered for use as a house. (Photo: Stewarts of Breacacha)

Cornaig – the school and schoolhouse. The school part is identified by the tall windows. (Photo: E. McGee)

and various organisations helped to set up many schools which were referred to as side-schools. The need for these side-schools continued until transport improved to a stage that enabled children to be taken by car or bus to the nearest village school. On Coll, there was a small side-school at Grishipol to cater for children in the area, and it was housed in a little corrugated iron building at the roadside near the farmhouse. This was built because parents rebelled against sending their children across the boggy moorland from the north coast road to Acha school. The five-year-olds just couldn't cope with that walk and, as a result, often didn't start school until they were nearly seven.

Since 1956 one school, in Arinagour's Carnan Road, has served all of the island's children of primary age, with many of them being bussed in from outlying areas. For their secondary education the children head for the mainland, returning during the main holiday periods and often at weekends.

Chapter 15

The Jewel Carriageway

A tale of **road** and line?

A STORY was told – and there was a fair ring of truth about it when first heard – of an interesting road maintenance technique some years back. On a hot summer's day, the two roadmen arrived at the required spot on Coll's East End road, opened a barrel of tar at the top of the adjacent slope and let the viscous substance begin to flow. Then they set off with their rods across the moor to Loch Fada, returning some hours later with a suitable catch for dinner. Before driving home, they put down a good load of small stones onto the tar which, by now, had more or less spread itself evenly down the full length of the slope. What the busy East End traffic – perhaps as much as a vehicle every half hour – did in the intervening period can only be guessed.

To begin with, there were nothing more than rough tracks on the island. When Johnson and Boswell stepped ashore in 1773 the direct track from Arinagour to the castles, now referred to as the West End road, did not exist. But they tell how this route was in its early stages of construction: 'The young Laird … has begun a road capable of a wheel-carriage. He has carried it about a mile, and will continue it by annual elongation from his house to the harbour [to Loch Eatharna]'. Johnson and Boswell took the long way round to the castles, firstly across the middle of the island to the Arnabost 'T' junction, then turning south-west made their way to the Great Plain and across it to Breacacha and the castles. They broke the journey a few times, the first stop being after 'about an English mile' at the house of Captain Lauchlan McLean. In that 'mile' they would have passed about ten houses dotted by the side of the track – all of them then would have shown plenty signs of life and yet now they are all reduced to about just one low rectangular course of stones.

Coll's dual carriageway on the East End road.
It is recommended that the direction sign be obeyed.

Progressively the tracks were improved, and by 1890 there were twelve miles of reasonable road on the island. In the same year the Council (the local authority) took over responsibility for their on-going upkeep. However, there was still a missing bit, a stretch that the East End people kept pressing to get built, and that was a road from the 'fishing gate' to the 'top' end of the island at Sorisdale. The Council kept responding that the expenditure would probably prevent the work. It was though eventually started and it was finished by 1911. Perhaps this campaign by the East Enders was part of a cunning plan since the island now had two road networks, the main twelve miles, the new bit, and – oops – a two-mile gap between them. In 1924 the gap was bridged between Gallanach and the 'fishing gate', and these two miles also became the Council's responsibility in the following year.

In 1938 the Council finally decided to tar-spray and chip all the listed roads, but with the outbreak of World War II it was years after hostilities ceased before the job was completed. There are some more recent small additions to the network such as Carnan Road in Arinagour, and the road to the new pier. In all, there are now about eighteen miles of surfaced road, and a few short stretches are still the typical old highland 'single-track-dual-carriageway' type of road. That is (a) one carriageway for the nearside (or offside) wheels; (b) a 'central reservation' of rough grass; (c) the other carriageway for the offside (or nearside) wheels. And, of course, on the East End road there is that wonderful jewel of real dual carriageway, all fifty yards of it, and its signpost telling you which way to go.

With only a few miles of road it is not surprising that there have only been a few driving incidents, such as somehow forgetting the important task of untying or unbolting a gate before actually driving through it! (The gates have been progressively replaced by cattle grids.) There has sadly been one fatality, and this was back in 1933 when a car inexplicably left the road and went into a peat bog. The driver, a local lad, was killed but the car's other occupants escaped with minor injuries.

We finish with the extract of an article written for the 1988 Coll Magazine:

> There are benchmarks along some of the roads, often covered with natural growth. Anyone interested will find the one on the brown flat rock as you turn into the Church of Scotland road quite easy to find. From there, going east, measure a mile on your car speedometer and you should be able to spot them all as far as Sorisdale.

If we're playing 'Hunt the Benchmark' instead of 'Hunt the Thimble' then, in 2014, the 'brown flat rock' and its benchmark was still easily found but, as for any of the rest, now there's a real challenge.

Chapter 16

First Port of Coll

Walking the plank?

A COMMUNITY which is dependent on a reliable sea link needs a harbour which is accessible at all stages of the tide, which is well sheltered against the excesses of wind and waves, and which has a substantial quay or pier. So, how does Coll fare? Around the year 1700 the Reverend John Fraser, an Episcopal clergyman, wrote: 'The coast of the Island is better than that of Tyrie or Gunna, for there entreth ane arme of the sea in the south and south-east side of it called Loch-fern [Loch-iern / Loch Eatharna] wher ships may saflie venture'. Later, in 1773, Johnson and Boswell arrived from Skye after a very rough voyage and recorded that: 'McLean of Col, a very active and skilful mariner, piloted us ... At last they spied the harbour of Lochiern and soon afterwards we got into it, and cast anchor ...There was in the harbour, before us, a Campbell-town vessel ... taking in kelp'. The description of Loch Eatharna as a place 'wher ships may saflie venture' needs some qualification, and for this we turn to an edition of the Clyde Cruising Club handbook: 'much exposed to southerly winds and a considerable swell sets in when the wind is in that quarter'. But, when the wind is in a favourable quarter and the sea is placid then many a yacht may be moored for the night at Arinagour. The number has been known to exceed forty!

While Loch Eatharna is first in terms of traffic there are many other little ports to be found, especially on the island's south-east coast, and some of them just served the few houses in the immediate vicinity. Located about two miles north-east from Arinagour, the two old stone jetties at Feisdlum have long been idle, other than for a real port in a storm when a local fisherman has judged it wiser to leave his boat there for the night and foot it back home to the village.

In the opposite direction, south-west from Arinagour, there is Fiskary with evidence of two old piers at the head of the bay and, given their proximity to the Tireemen's moss, it is likely that this is

Walking the plank between ferryboat and shore at the middle pier. The low tide is preventing access by the ferryboat to the steps on the other side of the pier. (Photo: Stewarts of Breacacha)

from where the peat was shipped out to Coll's neighbour. Further along the same coast is An Acarsaid Fhalaich (The Hidden Harbour) on the eastern side of the Fasach headland, and this was much favoured by An Cupair Collach (the Coll Cooper). He used it when he was on smuggling activities and trying to evade the customs men. He was such an expert seaman that the customs men were never able to catch him although they were well aware of his activities and hunted him continually. Many were the tales told at the ceilidh fireside of his ingenuity in dodging his pursuers.

Again on the south-west, is the harbour at Port-na-Luing, and it is of interest in that the remains of a pier which was being built for John Lorne Stewart can still be seen. Barley was being shipped out to the Campbeltown distilleries but, sadly, a severe storm did so much damage to the pier that Port-na-Luing remains very much today as it was then.

The Clyde Cruising Club handbook also tells us: 'There is no shelter to be had on the western sides of Coll or Tiree, and the whole of this coast is entirely exposed to the north and west. It is also much broken up and studded with dangers, both rocks and overfalls, and should be avoided.' And yet, across the island, on Coll's north-west coast are the harbours of Cornaig and Elleraig, and both of these were used by the East Coast fleet of boats which followed the herring shoals round Scotland.

Return to Loch Eatharna, the middle pier was built here mainly as a result of the destitution which followed the potato crop failures. Grain was sent to some Scottish communities in exchange for construction work, and Coll's pier was considered a worthy cause. In its 1850 report, the Destitution Committee stated that during that year, in return for 377 bolls of Indian cornmeal, oatmeal and seed, the people of Coll had constructed more of the road past Grishipol, had extended the West End road to the mill, and the pier at Arinagour had been erected. It was ninety feet long, forty feet broad, and twelve feet high. It still lacked one or two tiers in height, but was already considered useful.

In 1852, the *Cygnet* and the *Lapwing* began making journeys from Glasgow to this new pier. These were two of David Hutcheson's fleet of iron paddle steamers which had cargo as their main raison d'être but passengers were also carried. The size of these two paddlers – 77 feet long and with a 14½ foot beam – allowed them to use the attractive Crinan Canal and avoid the often difficult passage around the Mull of Kintyre. The canal took about a hundred miles off a typical journey to the islands.

As traffic to the islands grew so did the size of the ships, and in due course the ship owners resorted back to the more hazardous voyage round the Mull of Kintyre. Soon heading out to Coll from Glasgow one would see steamers like the *Dunara Castle*, sailing for a magnificent seventy-three years!

The middle pier met the island's needs for a time, since vessels of a considerable size could berth at the end of it and this was convenient for the speedy handling of livestock. There was a crane on the sheltered side where small boats were manually unloaded. The main disadvantage was that large deep-draught vessels could only berth on high tides – on an extremely low spring tide it is possible to walk in an almost straight line across the bay to Airidh Mhaoraich (the white cottage). The low spring tides were always something for the ferrymen to keep in mind – the ferry might need to be moved round early to the end of the pier or it would be high and dry when the mail boat came into the bay. Arrival back at the pier might mean literally walking the plank to get ashore dry – a substantial plank would be laid between the gunwale of the ferry boat and the shore on the seaward side. The water would be quite shallow but a fall would be so undignified.

As the visiting ships became ever larger, many islands and mainland ports were benefiting from improved berthing facilities. Coll, which had been agitating for an improved pier from as far back as 1879, just had to wait its turn. Eventually, in 1963, the preparatory work began – the construction of a stretch of road from the middle pier to the site of the new pier. The ferrymen of the day looked at the chosen site, shook their heads and told you where they thought it should have been – further out, they would say, probably best on Eilean Ornsay and link it to Coll by a short causeway.

Problem: how to build a new pier that will involve some large and heavy construction equipment, but there is not a pier currently available where such gear can be landed. Solution: land it on a beach! And so, with Angus Kennedy of Arinthluic acting as pilot, the landing craft *Abbeyville (L4041)* came into Breacacha Bay to offload. As Para Handy, captain of the 'finest vessel in the coastal tred', might have said: "Angus would ken every chuckie stane from the Cairns to Caolas" (would know every hazardous rock on the coastline). The equipment then trundled the few miles slowly and carefully to Arinagour, over a road which had been prepared for the occasion. With the visiting ships progressively becoming the Ro-Ro (Roll-on/Roll-off) type, there remained the last major upgrade to the new pier, the addition of the 118-feet link span, and this work was carried out in 1991/92.

It's 2008, and the *Hebridean Princess* cruise ship (formerly the ferry *Columba*) is at the new pier. The vehicle link span is stowed in an upward sloping position until needed. The stairway about halfway along on 'this' side was used mainly for the handling of livestock, especially on low tides. The large concrete dolphin at the outer end is an add-on to take the mooring ropes of the progressively longer ships. The gun from the *Nevada* keeps guard. (Photo: E. McGee)

Chapter 17

McLeans of Coll

... and of Grishipol and of Muck ... and of Germany

WHEN conversation revolves around the emigration of people from Scotland, there is a tendency to think of destinations such as the USA, Canada, Australia and New Zealand. What may be surprising is just how many McLeans there are of German birth and resident in Germany – some with distinctively Scottish forenames – and most of them with a strong link back to Coll, and from Coll back to Duart on Mull. When MacIlleathan himself, Sir Fitzroy Donald McLean, gathered many of the clan at Duart in 1912 to witness his banner once more flying over the castle after a gap of more than two centuries, there were McLeans present from Scotland, England, Ireland, Wales, USA, Canada, New Zealand – and Berlin. But, to begin at the beginning ...

According to tradition, the first McLean of anywhere was Gillean-na-Tuaigh, (Gillean of the Battle-axe) who flourished around the middle of the thirteenth century. He fought under Alexander III at the Battle of Largs and a grandson fought under Bruce at Bannockburn in 1314. Later, the McLeans settled in Mull and one of them, Lachlan Lubanach (Lachlan the Wily), became founder of the McLeans of Duart, the senior line of the clan.

There were four main branches of the McLeans: Duart, Coll, Lochbuie and Ardgour. The afore-mentioned Lachlan Lubanach had two great-grandsons, Hector (fourth of Duart) and his brother John (first of Coll). What now follows is a fast-forward run through the island's chiefs up to the sale of the Coll estate in 1856. Mostly there is only the briefest of quotable quotes.

Tourist Tips:

1. Not long after your ship leaves Oban on its way to Coll, watch out on the starboard (right) side for the conspicuous Lismore Lighthouse. The vessel will usually pass between it and Lady's Rock which has a small light on it. One McLean chief is said to have deliberately marooned his wife on the rock, with the expectation that she would not survive. She was fortunately rescued by passing fishermen and when McLean next dined at Inveraray Castle he was astounded to see his wife sitting at the top table next to her brother, the Duke of Argyll.

2. If you are puzzled by swirling waters in the area of Lismore Lighthouse and Lady's Rock (most obvious about half tide and even more so on spring tides), this is part of a tide race and the turbulence is accentuated by the shape of the sea-bed.

3. A little later, watch out for Duart Castle which stands proudly on the port (left) side as the ship enters the Sound of Mull.

Historian Tip:

The following list is probably correct chronologically. But, sources differ a little regarding inclusion, or exclusion, of a name as a chief (or laird). So, there may be some incorrect numbering down through the years and, for example, Hugh at 15th could perhaps be 16th.

1st chief: John Garbh (John the Rugged). Born in the early 1400s. A giant of a man, and cunning. As well as the lands of Coll and Quinish (on Mull), he held the lands of Lochiel and this resulted in feuding between the McLeans and the Camerons. He married a daughter of Fraser of Lovat and they had a number of children, including …

2nd chief: John. Born about 1425 and lived in Lochaber, but was killed by the Camerons. Two sons John and Hector and their mother were saved by another clan, the MacGillonies (or MacElonichs), who conveyed all three safely to Coll. It is said that there was a lintel on the old castle at Breacacha with a Gaelic inscription on it, translated as: 'If anyone of the clan MacElonich should appear before this castle, even though it were at midnight and with a man's head in his hand, he will be given shelter and protection from everyone but the King.'

3rd chief: John Abrach, son of the 2nd chief. While there is a suggestion that this John married and had a family, he was succeeded by his brother …

4th chief: Hector (? – c. 1593). Known as An Cléireach Beag (the Little Clerk)… a good poet… understood Latin. In the 1560s, feuding broke out between Duart and Coll, Duart insisting on Coll following him in all his private quarrels. Hector had a son John who was the first McLean of Grishipol. Later at Grishipol there was an Archibald McLean. He emigrated from Coll in 1753, and became a merchant in Danzig (now Gdansk in Poland) – we will call him Archibald I, but more of him later.

5th chief: Hector Roy (c. 1550 – c. 1595), a son of the 4th chief.

6th chief: Lachlan (c. 1582 – c. 1642), a son of the 5th chief. Had five children including Hector, who was the first McLean of Muck. While Lachlan was a youngster, a Nial Mòr (possibly a son of the 4th chief) acted as his guardian.

7th chief: John Garbh (c. 1604 – ?), a son of the 6th chief. A man of many fine qualities. Composed music and played the harp. The captain of an English ship which came to grief on the island saw him in the castle with a Bible in his hand and a harp at his side. Thinking of the Old Testament character, the captain remarked: "Is this King David restored to earth?"

8th chief: Lachlan (? – 1687), a grandson of the 7th chief. (Hector Roy, Lachlan's father, was a son of John Garbh the 7th chief but predeceased Lachlan.) Raised a company of men on his estates for service in Holland. During leave, he was drowned in the Water of the Lochy in Lochaber. Highly regarded at home and abroad.

9th chief: John Garbh, a son of the 8th chief. A youth of great promise. Died at the age of about eighteen when accidentally killed in Edinburgh.

10th chief: Donald (c. 1656 – c. 1729), another grandson of the 7th chief. Respected by all who knew him. Looked after the Coll estates while Lachlan was in the army.

11th chief: Hector (1689 – 1754), a son of the 10th chief. Tall, handsome, dignified, hospitable. A very amiable character in both private and public life. Built the new castle near the old one at Breacacha. He also kept a harpist, Murdoch MacDonald, who had been taught the instrument in Skye and in Ireland. Murdoch was perhaps the last harpist to be retained by a Highland chieftain.

12th chief: Lachlan, a son of the 10th chief. As all his male children died at a young age, the estate passed on to yet another brother …

13th chief: Hugh (? – c. 1786). Had eight children including Donald and Alexander Roy. This Donald was the 'Young Col' who met Johnson and Boswell in 1773 but who drowned in the Sound of Ulva a year later at the age of twenty-two. Johnson and Boswell tell us more:

> Mr Maclean of Col, having a very numerous family, has, for some time past, resided at Aberdeen, that he may superintend their education, and leaves the young gentleman [Donald], our friend, to govern his dominions, with the full power of a Highland Chief. By the absence of the Laird's family, our entertainment was made more difficult, because the house was in a great degree disfurnished; but young Col's kindness and activity supplied all defects, and procured us more than sufficient accommodation.

It was in 1771 that Hugh saw the start of building work on his splendid townhouse at 81 High Street in Old Aberdeen. The family were prominent in local affairs and Hugh himself was chief magistrate.

14th chief: Alexander Roy (? – c. 1835), a son of the 13th chief. Studied law but abandoned this on Donald's death in 1774. A captain in the Argyle Fencibles and later, a lieutenant-colonel in the Breadalbane Fencibles. Founded the village of Dervaig in his Quinish estate (Mull). On Coll, he had the rows of cottages built at Arinagour around 1812. A thorough highlander who treated his tenants with kindness.

15th chief: Hugh (1782 – 1861), a son of the 14th chief. Hugh served for a time in the Guards and became a lieutenant-colonel. He had a house built at Drumfin, near Tobermory on Mull. His estates, including Coll, were sold in April 1856.

....

Returning to the 'German' McLeans ... After Archibald I, who emigrated in 1753, there followed more McLean generations on the continent. Archibald II was born in 1772, and Archibald III in 1806.

McLean of Coll's townhouse in High Street, Old Aberdeen. Building work began in 1771. (Photo: E. McGee)

Archibald IV was born in 1842 and the *Celtic Monthly* tells how he achieved fame in the Franco-Prussian War. He rode boldly into Versailles with just a few men, threatening destruction if the town did not capitulate. The town officials imagined that there was a large Prussian force nearby and thousands of French troops surrendered. Archibald was awarded the Iron Cross and became known as the 'Conqueror of Versailles'.

Archibald V, born in 1876, visited Coll about 1896 along with an uncle. At the time of their visit there were about sixty McLeans living on the island and we may wonder how many distant cousin connections were established. The McLean family estate from 1825 to 1903 was at Szczerbięcin (south of Danzig and in modern-day Poland) where there was a large and well-equipped mansion house. Then, for over two decades the building was in use as a girls' school. In 1945, the whole area of Szczerbięcin was looted and from about 1950 the house was progressively demolished, leaving virtually no trace of its original grandeur.

Archibald McLean (IV) was born in 1842 (his Great Grandfather emigrated from Coll in 1753). In the Franco-Prussian War he was awarded the Iron Cross and became known as the 'Conqueror of Versailles'. (Photo: Celtic Monthly of 1897)

Chapter 18

Coll Box and Post Box

Please don't take the post box with you when you leave!

IT'S THE good old days, and someone is phoning from a 'chocolate box' village somewhere in rural England.

> Operator: "Number please?"
>
> Caller: "Coll 321."
>
> "321 – right, but what exchange?"
>
> "Coll."
>
> "Say again please. What exchange are you calling to?"
>
> "The exchange is *called* COLL! C - O - double L!"

… and sometimes after that …

> "Caller, do you perhaps know how to route the call to Coll?"
>
> "Probably first to Glasgow – then I'm not sure, but maybe Stirling next – then to Oban, and lastly via Scarinish on Tiree."

… and, as you might expect …

> "S – C – A – R – I – N – I – S – H"

While the call was being connected through the various exchanges an operator might happen to leave the line open, and one would hear 'Katie' in Oban asking 'Flora' in Tiree how her hens were laying these days. The old joys have now been largely replaced by mobile phones which, if you are looking for peace and quiet, work superbly on Coll. And, as at early 2014, they really do work in a few locations – at the top of Ben Feall or Ben Hogh, usually on or near the new pier, and on a good day at some other places.

Tourist Tips:

1. You have been dutifully advised.
2. Sorry, but as at July 2014, there is word of some forthcoming 'improvement' in mobile phone reception.

It was back in 1888 when the first telegraph communications were established with Coll, and about a decade later H. Rider Haggard made good use of them while he was staying as a guest at the new castle. He wrote: 'The telegraph, or rather the telephone, runs straight into the dining-room. Nothing ever brought the marvellous nature of this invention more home to me than the despatching of a message to Ditchingham [in Norfolk], five hundred miles away, and an hour or so later to be startled by a 'ting, ting' on the bell and rise to listen to the answer.'

In the early years things were rather prone to disruption, but the reliability and popularity of the telephone grew with time. Not every Coll household rushed to have a phone and there was not always a desperate need. If one only wished to keep in touch with a relative on the mainland say once a week, *and* without having to keep a supply of coins handy, *and* if one happened to live in the High Street within earshot of the village call box, then there was a very simple solution. On a weekend evening, when the cheap rate applied and the midges were not too numerous or ferocious, the odd door would be lying open in order to hear the ring of the incoming call, or someone would be standing waiting outside. To avoid a clash, there was presumably an agreement within the High Street about the timing of these calls, but the schedule would go adrift when the bay was full of yachts and too many crews came ashore to make contact with what *they* thought of as 'civilisation.'

Eventually the landlines and submarine cables became congested as the telephone traffic increased. In time, the island's exchange was automated. Then a microwave radio link was established and this brought a vast improvement in both capacity and quality. By the mid-1990s another joy was on the way out, with the removal of the telegraph poles and the burying of telephone lines – no longer would there be the pleasure of imagining you could actually hear the voices on the wires as the wind whistled around them.

There is always the letter for keeping in touch. The mail is not constrained by overloaded lines but it does have to contend sometimes with long winter storms when the ferry may decide it is not even worth leaving its sheltered Oban berth.

As far back as 1791 the Postmaster-General decided to establish a postal service to Tobermory on Mull. That town was still in its infancy but the plan was that this new service would improve things for Coll mail. For the next half century the carriage of mail seems to have been sporadic, due to the lack of a regular and reliable sailing between Mull and Coll – the New Statistical Account of 1843 reports that: 'There is a sub-post office to Tobermory, both in Tiree and Coll; but there has been no packet [a ship, not a parcel!] in either island for some years. Our means of communication are accordingly extremely irregular and uncertain, depending on any casual conveyance which may occur.' Gradually the ferry situation improved and since about 1900 the island has had a three-times-a-week schedule, as a minimum, with a corresponding frequency in mail collections and deliveries.

Probably the most interesting uplift of mail was in the autumn of 2001 when a complete and somewhat weighty post box was removed from a sturdy pole and taken from Coll. Unfortunately for the perpetrator, the postman was well on his rounds before the ferry got back to Oban, the box was missed, and an appropriate phone call was made to the authorities. The vehicles which had boarded at Coll that day were easily identified and the police officer's words at Oban might have been something like: "Right sir, now could we have a look inside the boot of your vehicle?"

Chapter 19

A Coll of Nature...

... and a Call of Nature

LET'S GET the 'Call of Nature' – a very respectable wee tale of course – out of the way first, and then we can enjoy the 'Coll of Nature' in comfort.

A Scottish clergyman was doing the rounds of his parishioners and made an afternoon visit to two elderly sisters. After yet another cup of tea he asked where he might 'wash his hands' and was shown to a rather nice guest bedroom which boasted – a washbasin! Another way of asking the same thing is to enquire about the location of the 'usual offices' or the 'facilities'. Yet again, on your ferry to Coll you might have seen a doorway labelled 'Taigh Beag', literally the 'little house'. When you have landed on Coll you may find that there is even another expression, thanks to a tale from one Coll worthy. This Collach had a certain reputation for cunningly coercing tourists into helping out in the field with his harvest. It might be likened to the classic tale of Tom Sawyer tricking a bunch of boys into thinking that the task – painting a fence – was fun, and Tom then had the afternoon to spend as he wanted to. The Collach also managed to get tourists involved with his harvest of the sea and they would find themselves struggling to haul up one lobster creel after another into a small open boat. This often meant a few chilly hours at sea and, after a time … Well, the bulb girls (mentioned elsewhere in these pages) were to be found working in the said boat and they put up a plea to 'go ashore' for the wee unsaid purpose. There is of course no copyright in the use of the phrase. So, when you are with some friends or family and sunning yourself on a beach, or perhaps enjoying a leisurely stroll across the machair, feel free to announce, "I'm just going ashore," with an explanation if really necessary, and everyone else will watch out for any 'intruders' as you head for a convenient wee nook or cranny. The phrase may well become universal but, remember, you heard it here first!

Okay now? Then we'll start on the Coll of Nature and talk first briefly about a very wee creature, the short-necked oil beetle (*Meloe brevicollis*). This little fellow put in an appearance on the island in 2009 and that's not bad considering it was believed to have become extinct in the UK more than sixty years earlier. The numbers recorded in 2014 showed a large increase over just a few years. Surely not a solution to UK oil supplies?

Even smaller than that little crawler is a creature well-known on the west coast of Scotland for its tiny but annoying bite – the midge. They can be a real nuisance and it is said that the best solution is to minimize the impact by trying to avoid the female of the species.

There is a more familiar 'ology', and visitors coming to Coll to enjoy the island's bird life are pointed to: *Birds of Tiree and Coll* by Bowler & Hunter. In addition, the website of the RSPB (Royal Society for the Protection of Birds) is worth a look, as the Society has a nature reserve at Totronald with a visitor information room. It was back in 1991 that the RSPB first acquired some land on Coll and it now manages over 1,000 hectares of the island.

It is the corncrake that usually attracts interest and it is towards the end of April that they start to arrive. Their 'crex, crex' is very distinctive and will be widely heard, but the bird can usually only be seen for a few weeks. They are very elusive.

Depending on the season, there are many other birds to be seen, and just some of them are the arctic skuas, auks, barnacle geese, dunlins, fulmars, gannets, godwits, golden plovers, hen harriers, lapwings, oystercatchers, ravens, redshanks, red-throated divers, redwings, rock doves, sanderlings, sandpipers, shags, shearwaters, skylarks, snipe, terns, turnstones, twites, and white-fronted geese. The sighting of a white-tailed sea eagle is quite possible – it will be over on a 'day trip' from Mull.

Visitors often ask about otters, seals and basking sharks. There is quite a good chance of seeing an otter on Coll. For the past few years there seems to have been a family in Loch Eatharna and it is best just to keep one's eyes open anywhere from the new pier right up to the head of the loch. Before leaving for Coll, a little bit of studying will also help, so that you may recognise otter signs such as the spraint (their droppings) and their footprints.

The elusive corncrake – on Coll. (Photo: A. McGee)

An otter feeding on a fish at the water's edge on Coll. (Photo: A. McGee)

Seals are quite numerous and will be found around the coasts. They do have a habit of following you with curiosity at a distance as you walk along a beach, but if you approach them closely on the rocks or sand they are quick to get away from you. And yet, they can surprise us. It has been known for one to break the habit and come out of the water and waddle across the beach right up to a camera-carrying visitor. Sort of, "I'm here for a photo op!" On a separate occasion, a teenager was slowly paddling a kayak close to the old pier when a seal surfaced and rested its chin on the bow. Paddling stopped. Then the seal dived and became quite visible because of the sandy sea

Tourist Tips:

Otters, seals, sharks, etc – expect the unexpected. If possible, walk or cycle since much will be missed from a speeding vehicle. Oh, and if you're thinking of having a dip in the water at Arinagour just when a fin is sighted close by, it will probably be a basking shark, but do ask if in any doubt!

bottom and the angle of the sun. The seal was spiralling below the surface in a sort of 'Marine World' display, but totally unrehearsed. The sequence of events was repeated many times as a small crowd gathered to watch this free performance.

Basking sharks have been seen in large numbers in recent years, especially on the north-west side of the island. They do also appear near and inside Loch Eatharna and you may even see a fin just a stone's throw from the old pier.

Chapter 20

THE WEE BUT AN' BEN

...and the big houses and the castles

"THE WEE but an' ben?" An old expression which is progressively dying out. "Come ben the hoose," your host/hostess would once have said and you would have been welcomed into the inner room/ the living room of a small single-storey house. The other room would have been a porch or maybe a bedroom, or even an area for the household's livestock. But, few 'buts' about it on Coll – just many small houses with nothing more than a single room.

House design and construction was largely dictated by the natural materials available in the vicinity. There would be four thick walls of large stones, the stones arranged to give the best fit possible and the gaps packed with soil. Timber for roof trusses depended mainly on what had been washed ashore from deck cargos or from shipwrecks. The roof thatch was usually held down by lengths of home-made rope which had a heavy stone tied at each end. The single doorway would be on the wall which faced away from the prevailing wind and the house itself would often be sited in as sheltered a spot as possible, such as behind a small hillock or rocky ridge. Windows? – maybe, but small and only providing a little light to the interior.

The inside? We learn much from the journal of Edward Daniel Clarke, a naturalist and mineralogist, who visited the Hebrides in the 1790s and entered some croft houses on Mull and Coll. In discussing the accommodation he writes about how pig-sties in England at least admitted fresh air while these Hebridean dwellings did not. Johnson and Boswell tend to focus more on the people who were living in such appalling conditions. Imagine the scene!

No carpet or floor covering, but maybe some fresh sand spread on the earth from time to time. One bed for the whole family, consisting of a mix of dry ferns and moss and running round the inside walls. Also on this one bed might sleep the family's animals – dogs, cats, and maybe even a pig. Above them, some rough timber beams would be 'home' to the chickens. Furniture is almost non-existent. Washed-up planks of wood provide rudimentary shelves on which sit some craggans, their home-made earthenware pottery. At the door, trying to get some light on his task, the father of the family is making heather rope which will be put to good use in holding down the roof thatch. An elderly female, perhaps a grandmother, is boiling herring guts for oil which will keep the lamps burning. The mother of the family is at her spinning wheel while some of the children are busily carding some more wool for her. For the household that had a dairy cow, there might be a butter churn inside. In the middle of the room is a peat fire, the smoke of which makes its escape through a hole in the roof. Outside there is no horse to pull a plough, since there is just a small patch of ground to be tilled, and nearly all the crofters turn over their soil with the cas-chrom – a foot plough. The cas-chrom's efficiency has been described thus: 'One man can turn over more ground with it in a day than four are able to do with a common spade.'

Clarke finishes his account with an interesting comment: 'If any one imagines happiness and contentment are strangers in these receptacles of abomination, they are much deceived; so relative is all human felicity. Surely, if anything can teach mankind the golden lesson of being contented with a small and peaceful competence, it is the spectacle of unfeigned satisfaction amidst poverty and want, such as this.'

Even when dire poverty became a thing of the past, it was still satisfying to live in an old house which was not yet supplied with 'mod cons' but was nevertheless sited not far from the lovely machair and, just beyond that, a beautiful sandy shore. Alan Villiers, a writer for the National Geographic Magazine, visited Coll about 1959 and was invited into an old thatched house that was situated six miles from the island's hub. Villiers described how the 'thatched roof was held down by a string of large stones garlanded round it, pendent from an arrangement of wire netting like a woman's hair net … the kettle sang upon the hob, and the neat little cottage reeked with the pleasant smoke of slow-burning peat.' An old couple – he had fought in the Boer War – sat on either side of the fire. The conversation drifted towards the subject of visits to town, i.e. to Arinagour.

> "Haven't been into town for fifteen years," chuckled the bodach (the old man).
> "That he hasn't. This will do for us!" added the cailleach (the old woman).

And, who would want to leave the beautiful solitude of much of the island for the relative bustle of its metropolis?

When one considers that Coll's population crept up towards fifteen hundred, the logical question is: "Where did they all live?" It is best answered by starting at the new pier and walking on the road towards the village. You will pass two ruined houses close by on the right – admittedly just the lowest course of stones and these being partially disguised by grass, bracken and heather. And, all over the island, especially near to the coast, there is a similar story – sometimes just a single building, sometimes two or three, and sometimes a little township. Possibly the most interesting old Coll township is that of Feall. Now there is no trace of it at all, and yet in 1776 it had a population of nearly one hundred. Its disappearance is due to years of blown sand – the people had no choice but to leave it.

From the wee but an' ben – Johnson and Boswell described it as: 'a hut, that is, a house of only one floor' – we move up to two-storey houses. As well as the new builds of recent years, there are quite a few around from the days when they would have been the homes of the tacksmen. The work to build them must have involved some sort of staging or scaffolding – probably of timber – and the construction took place in the days before health and safety was given due prominence. So, it was before the days of the important hard hats. When the Kilbride farmhouse was being re-built close to the West End road in 1880, a twenty-seven-year-old labourer from Arinagour was killed suddenly when a chimney head fell on him.

The best-known big house has to be the three-storey 'White House' at Grishipol. It was still inhabited when it was visited by Johnson and Boswell in 1773. Villiers heard one account of how it gained the huge crack that is still so obvious on the south end wall. The story told of gold having once been cached there and seekers after the treasure, digging with more energy than care, had undermined everything.

Then we come to the castles, although some might say that the new one more resembles a mansion house than a castle.

> … ane castell callit Brekauche, quhilk is ane great strength be reason of the situation thairof verie neir to the sea …

So says an account written in the late 1500s. The old castle at Breacacha, described in the 1930s as 'the most perfect and least altered example of a medieval stronghold in the Hebrides', does indeed sit very near to the sea. It is thought that the main tower-house part of it was built between 1425 and 1450, and there were additions and interior changes to the castle in the 16th and 17th centuries.

After the new castle was built, some parts of the old one were occupied for quite a time but eventually the roof of the main tower caved in, followed later by the floors below, and so the bottom level gradually acquired a large amount of guano. To a youngster who had

The two castles at Breacacha, probably in the 1930s. The old one, long before restoration, demonstrates 'the situation thairof verie neir to the sea ...' (Photo: Campbells)

some agility it was just the place to explore by climbing up to a level where there were rooms and passageways in the thickness of the walls. In the 1960s, its restoration for use as a residence began.

The new castle was built in 1750 and originally it fronted the sea. The Stewarts, who bought the Coll estate in 1856, made some alterations, plus the additions of an extra storey, a parapet and a porch on the landward side. Like its older neighbour, it became deserted but did not become a ruin.

Tourist Tip:

Be aware that neither castle is an empty derelict building for your close inspection. They are both now occupied residences and therefore please respect the owners' privacy.

Chapter 21

The Going gets Tough

'When the going gets tough the tough get going.'

SO THE saying goes. However, in the first half of the 19th century the toughness of the highlanders had been more than put to the test by famine, and those who did literally get going were generally the ones whose fare could be met.

Throughout the Highlands and Islands many places had been badly hit by the decline of the kelp industry in the 1820s. The next major disaster was the failure of the potato crop in 1835, with tens of thousands of folk being affected by it. There was no simple way out of the distressing situation. Emigration had a financial cost and many proprietors did not have the resources to help their tenants, since their pockets too had been affected when the kelp production ceased. The Gaelic-speaking crofters who contemplated a less distant move and who thought of trying the heavy industries of the Scottish Lowlands found themselves at some disadvantage – Irish labourers with more fluency in English had less difficulty in gaining the jobs.

Things deteriorated through 1836 and into 1837. The herring fishery failed and disease attacked the flocks in many places. Many entire parishes in the islands were without meal and had just enough potatoes to keep the people alive for a few weeks. There were no seeds to sow for the next year's crops. Their miserable life was maintained by collecting shellfish and seaweed at low tide, and by huddling together under a covering of dried ferns or rushes.

Then, help for some was to arrive from a quite unexpected quarter – Australia! The Rev J. Dunmore Lang of the Scots Church in Sidney arrived in the UK in 1836 and was soon aware of the famine. Lang knew of a source of funds in New South Wales and arranged for the offer of free travel to Australia to be intimated from church pulpits. The emigrants were required to be of a suitable age and of good character, to be vouched for, and to have skills which could be put to good use in their new homeland. This 'Bounty Ships' scheme, as it was known, resulted in four thousand souls being taken to Australia over a three-year period. On Coll in the church at Clabbach the islanders would have heard of the chance to emigrate

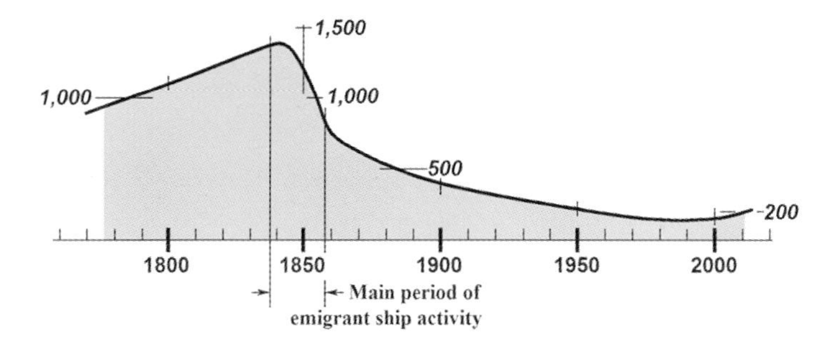

A graph of Coll's population over two centuries, derived from many sources. (Graph: E. McGee)

and the family discussions would have begun. At least they would likely already know a little about Australia – Lachlan MacQuarrie, Governor of New South Wales for some years, had been to the island a few times. But, to go or to stay – what a decision to make! To go might mean a household leaving behind a frail elderly relative, or siblings might be separated for good. To stay might mean a long time before conditions became any better. About eleven Coll households chose to leave in 1837 and began to prepare for the long voyage. One item that was sure to be packed was the family Bible – as well as its sixty-six printed books, there might be some valuable ancestry records hand-written on the flyleaves. When all was ready and when last farewells had been said, seventy-five men, women and children headed across to Mull and to Tobermory to join their ship.

The *Brilliant*, a well-appointed ship, arrived in Tobermory on the 15th September 1837. Over the next ten days the emigrants gathered from Coll, from Mull, from other islands and from some mainland communities, and became acquainted with the ship. On the 26th September a Gaelic sermon was given by the parish minister of Tobermory, and early the next day a steamer towed the ship through the narrow harbour mouth out into the Sound of Mull. The sails were set and a four-month voyage began, firstly heading westward into the open sea. Then, turning south, the Coll folk had the opportunity of a last lingering look at the island of their birth and the land of their forefathers before it finally disappeared below the horizon.

The *Brilliant* was not the first emigrant ship taking Coll families, nor the last. It happens though to be one of the more successful and well-documented voyages. There had been a small exodus from Coll in 1792, after a period of poor crops and little monetary return for cattle and kelp. Then, in 1819, the *Economy* sailed from Tobermory on a five-week voyage to Nova Scotia with some Coll families being counted in the 285 passengers on board. Conditions on Coll deteriorated in the 1820s with the price of kelp falling until it was no longer worth the effort to manufacture it. One islander with financial means had an interesting 'solo' emigration in September 1832, recorded as follows:

> **Emigration Extraordinary** – Mr Allan McLean, a respectable tacksman from the Island of Coll, sailed from Greenock on Saturday last for Van Diemen's Land [Tasmania] with wife and family … He fell in [not in the water!] at our Broomielaw [Glasgow's riverside], with a large schooner, the *John Dunscombe* from London, which he purchased, and paid in clear cash. He set sail with her, as before stated, on Saturday last, taking none but his own family, a mate, and three sailors! Mr McLean was in a respectable way in Coll, and gave up his farm much against the laird's will – but his eldest son having been in Van Diemen's Land several years, and prospering, induced the aged parents to give the junior members of the family the same footing.

Other ships sailing in the 1830s from Tobermory and carrying folk from Coll were the *British King* on the 28th October 1838 and the *George Fyfe* on the 15th September 1839, both heading for Australia.

For those that were left on Coll there was yet more hardship to come. In 1846 the crops failed again and much of the population was on the verge of destitution, barely surviving on shell fish for food. Westminster became aware of the severity of the situation that

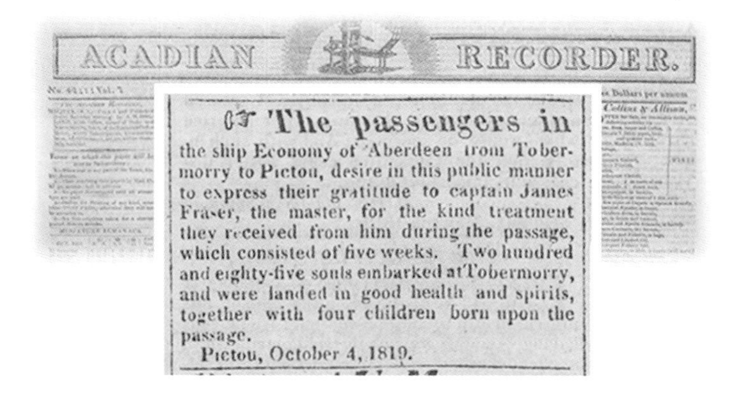

ACADIAN RECORDER.

☞ The passengers in the ship Economy of Aberdeen from Tobermorry to Pictou, desire in this public manner to express their gratitude to captain James Fraser, the master, for the kind treatment they received from him during the passage, which consisted of five weeks. Two hundred and eighty-five souls embarked at Tobermorry, and were landed in good health and spirits, together with four children born upon the passage.

Pictou, October 4, 1819.

A notice of appreciation from the passengers of the ship *Economy* appears in an 1819 edition of the *Acadian Recorder*. There were a few Coll families on board.

prevailed in the Highlands and Islands, and early in 1847 Royal Navy warships loaded with rice and meal sailed from the south of England. Their destinations included Tobermory, and from such distribution points the supplies were delivered to various locations by smaller ships. There was also some direct financial help provided by a body called the Highland Destitution Committee.

During the 1850s another set of ships set sail for Australia, carrying islanders from Coll and other places, but this time the British departure port was Liverpool. At least five ships had Coll folk on the passenger list. In 1852 there were the *Marmion* and *Flora McDonald*. The *Edward Johnstone* and *Hornet* sailed in 1854. In 1857 the fifth ship was the *Persian*, but a year earlier the main Coll Estate had been sold and the new laird was John Lorne Stewart of Glenbuckie. Within a few years of Stewart's purchase, things were to change significantly for those who had not emigrated.

The *Persian* left Liverpool on 26th July bound for Hobart on Tasmania, with 325 on board. Just twenty-two days into the voyage, typhus fever broke out and ten people had died before she reached her destination. The *Persian*'s arrival at Hobart on 31st October 1857 created considerable local alarm, and for five days the Tasmanian authorities deliberated on what to do. Recruiting a local doctor to assist the victims was extremely difficult. The first one requested an annuity to his wife in the event of his death and was refused. The second one pulled out at the last moment and it was the third one who took the job. Even the pilot who boarded the ship without first making an appropriate enquiry was detained until the ship was released from quarantine. The solution was to have a steamer tow the ship about thirty miles to Impression Bay (now called Premaydena) and to quarantine her passengers and crew at a former convict probation station. In the thirteen Coll families who sailed, there were nine deaths. These included John McLean, aged twenty-six, who died on board the ship and was buried 'over the side'. By 17th November the danger was over and the ship was cleared to return to Hobart. This was especially hard for one man in Hobart who had waited for some months to be re-united with his wife. While the authorities were deliberating in the early days of the crisis he was only able to look out at the ship where, on board, his wife was dying.

On Coll, Stewart was developing a reputation as a tough person to deal with and there are accounts of rents being collected from his tenants while a revolver lay beside him on the table. He had raised the rents to a level that the crofters could not meet and they were effectively forced to move, but to where? Rather unusually, the last single large Coll migration was neither emigration nor immigration. During a single weekend in 1861 many families trekked north-eastwards from the West End and from the middle part of the island into the Cornaig Estate, which was not Stewart territory. Colin Campbell, the proprietor of Cornaig, was sympathetic to their plight and had agreed to give them some land. The move was like an exodus, with the adults and the children driving their cattle on ahead of them, and ponies carrying their goods. To begin with, the families had to make do with basic shelters and then, one at a time and in a communal manner, houses were built.

From then on, the island's population continued to decline slowly and steadily, and it was well over a century later before the incomings overtook the outgoings.

Chapter 22

Flora and the Bulb Girls

WHAT more can one say here when there is a recent and relevant publication to get hold of: *Wild Flowers of Coll and Tiree* (Cinquefoil Publishing, 2008). But Coll's wild flowers have been around for a long time, and visitors and residents have marvelled at, and commented on, the island's rich spectacle over the centuries:

> 1764 – John Walker writes of: 'the most beautiful embroidered carpet that the earth perhaps is anywhere covered with.'
> 1803 – The Hon Mrs Murray of Kensington describes: 'a plain thickly covered with a wild geranium of the finest purple colour I ever saw.'
> 1810 or thereabouts – John MacCulloch, a geologist, writes in letters to Sir Walter Scott: 'But its ordinary flowers, if they do not rival those of our gardens in variety and splendour, are by position, contrast, and numbers, not less captivating to the eye; while the whole atmosphere is perfumed by their fragrance … it was an enamelled carpet of indescribable gaiety.'
> 1937 – Hector MacDougall says: 'The appearance of the Machair Mor in July when the wild geranium and other summer flora are in full bloom is a sight seldom equalled in beauty and certainly never excelled anywhere else in the Hebrides.'
> 1948 – The Scotsman's Nature Notes section has: 'Perhaps the finest sight of all is the carpet of wild geranium which covers the machair sloping down to the white sands of the Traigh Feall. The emergency landing strip is here, and surely nowhere else do aircraft touch down on a sward so starred with flowers.'

Tourist Tip:

Please leave this carpet of wild flowers in as beautiful a condition as you find it. Vehicles can do a lot of damage!

It was in the 1950s when there was a significant floral addition to the island, and the press, especially the farming press, ran headlines such as:

> HOLLAND IN THE HEBRIDES
>
> Bulb Growing gives the island farmers a new crop

The bulb industry on Coll was written of in glowing terms: '… already there is a most excellent hotel, signs of a tourist trade and a hostel to which a number of young ladies are coming in order to harvest the bulbs. It is on such developments that the island's future depends.'

The idea for the commercial growing of flower bulbs in the Hebrides surfaced in 1952, and within a few years there was enthusiasm for the industry on several islands. It took root on Coll at three locations: Breacacha, Gallanach and Grishipol. The Gallanach bulbs, nearly all daffodils, came mainly from Holland and were planted around August for flowering in late February. The summer months were when there was most work on the bulbs but the rest of the farm had to be kept going at the same time. So, for its supply of extra hands, the island began to be invaded annually by the 'bulb girls'. The girls will tell much of the story:

> I can well remember the excitement of the door of the *Claymore* being swung open and seeing the wee red ferry boat bobbing towards us. Originally there were about twelve of us bulb girls, mostly students. We were taken up to the old school above the village by tractor and trailer. This was our home for the next four weeks and very adequate it was too.
>
> We worked on weekdays from 8 am to noon and 1 to 5 pm, and on Saturdays just until noon. The day began around 7 am and after a quick wash (one bathroom/lavatory for twelve of us) and a hurried breakfast we clambered onto the old trailer. Flat out we went, with the trailer swaying wildly, passing cattle on the road – dodging the flying cowpats – then a right turn at Arnabost ... over the hill to the sight of the sea and Gallanach and the bulb field.
>
> We tumbled out of the trailer and made our way to a line of bulbs, sharing it between us. We could see the white roots of the bulbs in the sandy soil and had to dig them out with our hands, put them into baskets, and tip these into wooden trays. We worked either bending down or squatting. The work was not heavy, but the monotony was great!
>
> At lunchtime we all rushed down to the beach with sandwich tins and a flask of strong tea. Nearly everyone changed and went into the freezing Atlantic. When there were breakers, we were buffeted so much that we didn't feel the cold. Then another quick change, and a lovely picnic lunch.

It is also told that an early swimming occasion on a hot dusty day was rather impromptu, and so:

> "Anyone for a swim?"
> "But we've not come prepared."
> "Should be okay. Most holiday-makers will be along the coast on Torastan."

Time off for the bulb girls at the 'hostel', i.e. the old school. (Photo courtesy of H. Parsons)

The bulb girls at work in a Gallanach field. (Photo courtesy of H. Parsons)

And, as a result, a small postcard-sized notice from an ecclesiastical source appeared in the shop window, and it had some wording to the effect that such a display was not to be repeated!

The girls continue:

> At 5 pm the drive home with the sight of the old school over the hill, and tea – lots of it. Then the best part of the day: the long evenings until midnight – peace and quiet, exploring the island or meeting Coll friends, sometimes a ceilidh, a 'fillum' or a dance – all the social life that made the dull work worthwhile. I was a bulb girl for a number of years and during all that time the hospitality and kindness we received from all the Collachs was amazing.

Unfortunately this innovative enterprise did not last long – the bulbs were decimated by disease. Now when you visit the island you may see hosts of golden daffodils in some remote corners and they will tell you of the days when, as the bulb girls would say: "We laboured in the hot sun, swam in the cold sea and danced the summer nights away."

Chapter 23

Three Men 'n' a Boat

THE STEAMER *Hebrides* served Coll for well over half a century and for part of that time she was captained by three Collachs. So, her inclusion in these pages seems justified. She was the second ship to have been designed by the famous G. L. Watson for Messrs John McCallum & Co. Watson's *Hebridean* of 1881 remained with McCallum until 1917 but, with the newer and larger *Hebrides* on the scene, she was often surplus to West Highland requirements and could be found at places such as Bideford (for Lundy Island trips), Bristol, Ilfracombe, Isle of Man, Liverpool, Plymouth, St Helier (Jersey), and Sainte-Brieuc (Brittany). John McCallum himself was tragically drowned in 1902 at St Helier when he was boarding the *Hebridean* late one evening.

Getting back to the subject matter of *Three Men 'n' a Boat* and first, the boat – sorry, *ship* – built by the Ailsa yard at Troon in 1898. The specification for the *Hebrides* makes for interesting reading, with delights such as:

> To be built … with full poop and topgallant forecastle … Lightly rigged as a two-masted fore-and-aft schooner [Seems as if G. L. Watson couldn't get the idea of sails out of his mind. But, among his many designs was the graceful *Britannia*, possibly the most successful racing yacht ever built.] … Bell – 14 inches of bell metal, of rich tone, and with the ship's name engraved on it [And that engraved bell survives today, prominently on display aboard the third *Hebrides*.] … Frets on each side of skylight beams to hold flower-pots … Sofa seats covered with the best crimson Utrecht velvet.'

In 1902, a Rev Roderick Lawson gave a lecture about a journey aboard the ship. The lecture became a booklet and in it he writes: '… sixty passengers … and every berth was occupied … the food was plentiful and wholesome … The chief drawback is the poor character of the sleeping accommodation … I slept in a lower berth, and it was impossible to get into it or get out of it with any sense of dignity, or even self-respect!'

Over half a century after her first appearance on the water the ship's swansong was a cameo role in the Ealing Studios 1954 classic comedy *The Maggie*. Mr Pusey, played by Hubert Gregg, is sent down to Kingston Dock in Glasgow to check out the seaworthiness of the ship that is going to carry a 'most valuable cargo' for his boss. By mistake, and to the delight of the puffer *Maggie*'s crew, he walks right past their decrepit rusting little vessel, steps onto the gangway of the adjacent *Hebrides* and, after a most cursory glance at the wrong ship, assures himself: "There are no concerns on that score."

Now for three of her captains. From the start of the ship's service and for over two decades, the skipper was John Campbell, born on Coll in the early 1850s and brought up in the West End at Caolas. A grandfather had been a ferryman at Caolas and an uncle worked on the same ferry. So, the sea was in his blood. George Blair, the ship's purser of many years, put the stories of some early voyages into print. He tells of an incident involving Captain Campbell which occurred near the Isle of Skye during the 1914–1918 war:

Our course after leaving the Port of Soay is almost invariably between Soay and Skye ... the usual route. The difference of distance between this route and that outside of Soay is really negligible. When I found Captain Campbell taking the unusual route, I asked him what had made him do so.

"I really cannot tell you," he replied. "It simply came up my back to do so."

When next we put into Soay we were informed that a German mine had stranded on the beach there. This mine must have been in or pretty near our customary path when Captain Campbell for no apparent reason chose the outer route. Now was this mere coincidence or the act of the little cherub sitting up aloft who presides over the destinies of mariners?

Or, thirdly, and probably not known by Blair, was it because the captain took as his bride a Uist girl who is said to have told him: "If you marry me then no ship under your command will ever come to grief" – a prediction nicely echoed in an obituary: '... the various vessels which came under his command were severally sailed with conspicuous success and practically without mishap due to navigation.'

The second Collach was John McKinnon from Cornaig. He appears in some 1923 film footage of the *Hebrides* taking supplies and tourists

The ss *Hebrides* anchored in Loch Eatharna, with a Coll ferryboat coming alongside at the aft doors. The insets show – left to right – the ship's bell, now displayed on board the *Hebrides (III)*; Captains John Campbell, John McKinnon and Donald MacFarlane. (Main photo: R. Sturgeon)

from Glasgow to St Kilda. St Kilda was on the ship's schedule roughly every four weeks, but only in the summer months, and tourists were enticed by advertising material which told them of a: 'Splendidly fitted steamer, lighted by electricity, Superior Accommodation, Bathroom, etc.' As for the pull of St Kilda: 'During the Season extended trips are made to this most interesting and romantic island, also to beautiful and wild Loch Roag, Lewis, when passengers are given facilities (Weather Permitting) for landing'. As well as running the ship, Captain McKinnon would chat with the regular passengers – many known to him – and the tourists. The tourists would find themselves visiting between ten and fifteen islands on their seven to eight day voyage, but many calls were short and with little time for sight-seeing. Compared with the huge cruise liners of today, there was little in way of organized on-board entertainment and it was quite normal for the tourists to arrange their own amusements, with some music or recitations and maybe even an impromptu concert. On the last evening as the ship was on the homeward leg back to Glasgow there would likely be a toast by the 'senior' tourist to the captain and the officers.

Appearing in the same 1923 material as Captain McKinnon is her third Collach, Donald MacFarlane, known to some as *Domhnull-na-Heb*. At the time of the film he was a seaman and some years were to pass before he had 'Captain' before his name. Donald served on the *Dunara Castle* as well as the *Hebrides* and also made the trips out to St Kilda where he knew most of the inhabitants. In the narrow channel leading to Loch Eport on North Uist he sometimes brought the *Hebrides* alongside a conveniently shaped rocky coastline which had an ample depth of water, and where cattle and sheep could therefore be driven over a gangway directly on to the ship's deck, thus saving the drovers miles of difficult overland travel to a pier. (Such a loading technique was not new. It is known that Captain John McCallum took the *Hebridean* close in to the rocks at Tiree, which at the time did not have a good pier, and loaded horses by a gangway.) Early in 1946 Donald heard that he had been appointed as a Member of the Order of the British Empire for 'meritorious Sea Service in the Merchant Navy'. When he died in 1947 it was written in the press that: 'He typified in courtesy, bearing and efficiency all the best qualities in Hebridean seamanship than which no higher praise can be earned by anyone.'

Chapter 24

Tales of Rod and Line

The other John Knox

IN 1923 Seton Gordon wrote of how: '…on the horizon, as often as not, one could see the herring drifters rise and fall upon the swell that is rarely absent from the Coll banks.' And these fishing banks to the west of the island were well known for the quantity and variety of catch to be found there. So, for an island location such as Coll, it may seem odd than fishing was never a key part of the local economy.

It was back in 1787 that a John Knox (not the John Knox of the Reformation era) made a lengthy journey around the Scottish coast and then laid out his ideas for the fishing industry. Knox proposed the establishment of fifteen new villages in the Hebrides, with others throughout the Highlands. The list of locations included West Loch Tarbert (on the Kintyre peninsula), Plockton, Lochinver, Jura (the small isles location), Tobermory, Kirkapol on Tiree, Loch Eatharna on Coll, Portree, and Isle Oransay on Skye. As well as publishing his detailed and costed plans, Knox wrote to the various land owners including McLean of Coll. His reasoned that, where a small fishing village was set up, the value of lands would rise and it would therefore be in the interest of the proprietor to gift a certain portion of ground for such a village. Knox also argued that the Hebridean weather was not often the best for producing crops, claiming that every third year on average was a year of famine.

Some landlords who took Knox's ideas seriously and who tried to set up villages found it hard to get their tenants to switch from farming to fishing. To the tenants, their land was an important thing and McLean of Coll encountered this same stumbling block. The farmers would also be contemplating the problem of fish curing without an adequate supply of salt, the expense of buying boats, hooks and lines, and the winter storms that could bring both danger and damage. McLean tried to persuade them by planning to bring some expert fishermen from Shetland and settle them on Coll, and so to pass on their skills at catching and curing fish. Even this did not help to stir local interest.

So the Coll Banks were fished mainly by boats from further afield and in the second half of the nineteenth century the harbours at Cornaig and Elleraig were busy places, so busy that in 1896 a plea reached Westminster for the positioning of a buoy outside of Cornaig, a navigational aid much favoured by the Secretary of State for Scotland but which never materialised.

Fishing by the islanders has however been around on Coll, albeit in a small way, for a very long time and it is thought that the two causeway-like walls that cross the head of Loch Eatharna might be fish traps, built to effectively capture fish behind them as the tide went out.

There are many boat noosts round Coll's shores, mostly on the south-west side of the island. A noost is a place where a boat is drawn up out of the water. To make a noost, any large stones at the water's

Cornaig Harbour in the East End. This harbour and nearby Elleraig were busy places when many boats, especially those from the east coast of Scotland, were following the herring shoals. (Photo: E. McGee)

edge were moved away to the side, leaving a clear and narrow stretch of sand that would not damage the underside of a boat as it was dragged up to the high tide mark. You will quite likely find a single noost adjacent to many a shore-side house, but the north side of Gortan bay boasts three of them. Each noost tells of a small boat in use for fishing, and the catch was often for baiting lobster creels. A secondary function of the islander's boat was communication – a slightly choppy sea was likely to make for a much easier journey than the rough track from the islander's home to the village, and it was the ideal route if the boat was carrying lobsters for shipment off the island via the middle pier and the ferryboat.

Now, in the early years of the 21st century, there are a few boats setting out regularly from Arinagour and returning with lobsters, velvet crabs, and crayfish, and the catch goes off to the mainland – and beyond? It probably can't all be attributed to Knox's publication – *A Tour through the Highlands of Scotland and the Hebride Isles in 1786* – but it is a fishing industry, and it is part of the island economy. It just didn't need a new village.

Chapter 25

Fun and Games

LIKE many a highland place, the Coll islanders are very capable of having great impromptu ceilidhs. But, they also have their large and more planned events. There is the Isle of Coll Show every August, and the 100th such event will come round in the year 2021. The content of the show has changed over the years. For example, in the 1930s you would have seen some typical heavyweight events such as throwing the hammer, and in the 1960s there was a tractor driving competition.

Nowadays, in 2014 to be precise, there are so many things in which you can participate. The children, including visiting children, are well catered for, with two categories just for them. Out of 140 separate competitions, and just selecting one from each of ten categories, you can see the following, which looks almost like a set of clues for a cryptic crossword: Most Outrageous Vegetable, 6 Eggs (other), Table Centre, Interesting item found on the shore, Cherry Cake (Men only), Best Old Dog (any breed), Dressed Up Vegetable (9 & over), Hand-made Birds Nest, Best Rocker or Hillbilly Outfit (8 & under), Cross Bred Gimmer (home bred).

Until effectively cancelled by the withdrawal of transport connections, there was the annual island 'evacuation' over to Mull on a July Thursday for the Tobermory Games. As well as actually going up the hill to the Games, i.e. for those who managed to get past the Mishnish Hotel, there was the rare opportunity to do some business and shopping and be back home on Coll in the same day. What made these trips so rewarding was to see Coll's highland dancers regularly bringing back a good amount of silverware.

Tourist Tip:

If you somehow manage to get over to Tobermory for the Games, *and* if you pop into the Mishnish for a dram or ten, *and* you remember to stop at the butchers for some liver for the next evening's meal, *and* you put the paper bag containing the liver into a trouser pocket, *and* you fall heavily on the steep road up to the Games field then, when a medic shows up, do remember to explain that the blood soaking the trouser leg is probably not your own.

The Coll Show as it was in the 1920s. The location was near the Lodge at Arinagour. (Photo: Stewarts of Breacacha)

Golf? Yes, the island has a course. H. Rider Haggard tells how in the late 1800s an eighteen-hole course was being set out at Breacacha. During work on one of the greens, four skeletons, one being that of a child, were discovered buried beneath the turf. Perhaps not surprisingly, the green was located at Croc-na-Crochadh (Hangman's Hill), close to the Garden House. The Breacacha course only lasted for a decade or so and it was in the 1930s that a start was made on a nine-hole 2,800-yard course at Cliad, with claims that the sand hills would make fine natural bunkers and that two very sporting short holes were to be included. The current arrangement of fairways and greens may be somewhat different from the 1930s version, but with two tees for each hole it provides enough variation to regard it as an eighteen-hole course. In the high season – we're talking June/July/August – you may find a 'packed' programme of events, and for 2014 these were advertised as:

The Members' Cup (The Club Championship) over four days.
The Coll Open, a one-day open event for Juniors, Ladies and Gents.
The Campbell Scramble, a one day event for over 16s.
The Vita Stableford, a one-day open competition.

A golfer at Cliad in the early 1930s. It begs the question: Is he is going to *tee* off or *tea* off. (Photo: Campbells)

Clearly, one can't expect to see television gantries and cameras at the Coll Open but there will be a plentiful supply of rabbits showing an interest in the game, especially to see how many balls end up well inside a burrow. The holiday-makers visiting the Cliad course for the first time may be on the hunt for the club house and they can hunt as much as they like – it's a good walk to the nineteenth, to the hotel! They should head for the hotel at some point anyway and pay the fees for their game.

Also in the summer, various other activities may appear on the local calendar of events, with the tourists much in mind. There may be organised wildlife events, fishing competitions, a musical workshop, ceilidh nights with top class bands, a quiz night, a bingo night, a beach football day, and new for 2014 is a possible petanque tournament.

There is a Coll Sailing Club with a few dinghies available for use in the summer months. Of course, there is a rescue boat, plus buoyancy aids and safety helmets. Details may change with time, but visitors can check the notice board on the side of boat trailer.

The island's half-marathon is now a well-established August event and typically attracts over four hundred competitors spread across the full half-marathon run, the 10k run, the 5k run, the children's 1k run and the half-marathon walk. Almost overnight the island's population more than doubles. The full course runs round the south-west of the island with the full run/walk and the 1k starting on the new pier. Now, what happens if a member of the pier staff has accepted the role of a starter and he's ready with his synchronised watch to give a countdown of "10, 9, 8, 7, 6 ..." and just at that very moment there is the ferry arriving behind schedule and her mooring ropes need his attention? The answer is that the start has a touch of typical highland humour. The other start points, for the 10k and 5k, are located round the course to achieve a common finishing line in the village at An Cridhe.

The island's population is 200, give or take. So, it's quite amazing that the island can raise a football team – with substitutions? – a cricket team, and two shinty teams. Clearly some islanders are skilled in more than one sport. *Two* shinty teams? Yes, for the annual New Year's Day match at the Cliad 'stadium' and the teams are, rather loosely, the West-Enders and the East-Enders.

A runner in the half-marathon is now on the 1¼ miles of sand track through the dunes between Totronald and Ballehogh. The remainder of the course is on the road. Just 5½ miles to go! (Photo: 'Stevie')

As if three sports are not enough, some islanders have demonstrated their hunger for very strenuous athletic enterprises in aid of good causes. In 2012, twelve swimmers – some from Coll and some from the mainland – took part in a relay event from Ardnamurchan Point to Sorisdale, this being in aid of Macmillan Cancer Support. Then, in 2014, nine cyclists – again, some from Coll and some from the mainland – took part in a gruelling seven day event entitled 'North of the Fault'. This was a route of 811 miles, with over 54,000 feet of ascent, in the Highlands of Scotland lying to the north and west of the Great Glen fault line. The charity benefitting in this case was Mary's Meals.

And in the winter? As well as the shinty, the tourist spending a few weeks on the island over the festive season may be fortunate enough to 'take in' a pantomime. Yes, a home-grown am-dram night on Coll, but not an annual event. The most recent and most excellent production from the Coll amateurs was called 'Sno Right and the Seven Dwarfs'. Coll surely does spoil you with its variety of fun and games!

Chapter 26

Lachlan na Gaidhlig

IN THE 1970s on the Isle of Lewis some bi-lingual islanders were enjoying a good evening's 'chin-wag' round a peat fire and all speaking in their native Gaelic. One of them asked the others if they would mind having the television switched on for the late evening news [which would be in English], as there was likely to be an item of interest. Not long after the news had finished and the set switched off, there was a sudden exclamation from one of the group: "Why are we all speaking in English?" Ah, the power of the media, especially television!

It was round about 500 AD that Gaelic became established as a language in Scotland, and its influence progressively grew until it peaked between the tenth and thirteenth centuries. The period of the Norse invaders did not kill it off, and on Coll it continued as the main language right up until about 1850. Then the introduction of English-speaking dairy farmers from the mainland was probably the start of its decline on the island.

John MacCulloch, writing in the early 1800s, gives other reasons for the advance of English into the Gaelic stronghold of the Hebrides: 'A consequence of communication between the natives and the Lowland fishermen and traders; and of the voyages and journeys of the former to the Low country ... The steam boats export it from Greenock.'

It is now a few decades since there was any Scottish person still alive who had been brought up with Gaelic as his/her first tongue and yet was unable to converse in English. Such an inability might however be feigned to one's advantage. Some years ago, a Hebridean driver was taking an articulated lorry load of shellfish to market in Spain. At one continental border post it was routinely expected that some money might quietly change hands, in order that the customs officials would then speedily complete the necessary paperwork for the crossing. The driver was clearly fluent in some language that was 'foreign' to the officials and, equally clearly, English was 'foreign' to the driver. There was some shrugging of shoulders and free passage was granted.

One of the most distinguished Gaelic-speaking Collachs was Lachlan McLean (1798–1848) from Arnabost. He records his own genealogy as: 'Mac Iain mhic Lachin mhic Iain mhic Dhomhuil mhic Ruari mhic Eachin mhic Neil mhic Challum mhic Lachin mhic Iain–Garbh,' and this shows that he was the eleventh in direct male descent from John Garbh the first McLean of Coll. His early education was in Coll, under a teacher by the name of Ebeneezer Davidson, and when he moved to Glasgow in 1821 he was taught Hebrew by a Jewish Rabbi. Most of his time was spent working in a hosiery shop and, when his employer retired, Lachlan then carried on the business in the premises until 1841.

His writing was effectively a secondary activity but his literary skill was such that in one tribute it was said he could write Gaelic as if he knew no English, and English as if he knew no Gaelic. Boldly going where possibly no-one had gone before, Lachlan set out to prove in *Adhamh agus Eubh* (MacLachlan & Stewart, 1837) – just one of his published works – that Scottish Gaelic was not only older than Hebrew but that it was the very first language ever, the language of Adam and Eve.

Now, hold up one hand. Let's be generous, *both* hands. The number of fingers will approximate to the number of fluent Gaelic speakers who can nowadays give Coll as their home address.

Chapter 27

Let's Face the Music ... and Dance

Lochaber no More, or bagpipes no more?

IT HAS been said – rather unkindly – that it would great if the business of plate tectonics got a bit of a move on. Then perhaps the plate holding the Highlands and Islands might split off from the rest of Scotland, possibly along the line of the Great Glen, and drift away into the Atlantic or the Arctic Ocean, and hopefully taking with it at least half of the country's bagpipe players. We shall ignore this suggestion and move on.

In 1773, Johnson and Boswell were: '... at Col under the protection of the young Laird [the laird's son, Donald] ... The bagpiper played regularly ... and he brought no disgrace upon the family of Rankin.' The piper that they heard was Neil Rankin and some sources have it that Neil's wife Catherine was directly descended from a McLean of Coll and therefore was not too distant a relation of the laird's son Donald. But, bagpipe music was at least alive on the island even if the law was being broken – after the 1745 Jacobite rising, the playing of it was proscribed, and it was not allowed again until 1782 because it had been regarded as an instrument of war.

Rankin was almost certainly entertaining Johnson and Boswell with the *Ceol Mòr* (the 'Big Music' or piobaireachd). Seton Gordon, the writer, naturalist and piping judge, wrote in 1923 about the great Coll piper John Johnston (1836–1921). Gordon's narrative is so vivid that a lengthy extract is justified here:

> The old piper's croft stood on the western side of the island. Within a stone's throw of the door the long Atlantic waves broke with a deep, soothing sound upon a strip of golden sand ... It was a peaceful spot, and of a clear summer's night the westering sun bathed all the long chain of the Outer Hebrides, and shone ruddy on the conical heights of Rum and on the Skye hills behind them.
>
> Although the old piper was still vigorous and his fingers retained their cunning, it was never easy to persuade him to take down his ancient chanter from his shelf. He had little patience with the young players round him, for they contented themselves with the music of march, strathspey and reel, which the veteran considered immeasurably inferior to the Ceol Mor, or Big Music, which he played so well in his younger days. The old piper was positive that the old masters never demeaned themselves by playing marches and reels. Indeed, according to him, they were never permitted to do so, and the Chieftain of Coll nearly dismissed one of the best pipers he ever had when, returning unexpectedly to the castle at Breacacha, he heard that piper (thinking his master was out of earshot) playing a march for his own gratification.
>
> It was, as I have said, no easy matter to persuade him to play, but of a December's evening, when the wind moaned without and when the peat fire burned brightly in the small room,

> the veteran's interest in far-off days would be roused by the first notes of his chanter. At first he would play haltingly, as though his old fingers were finding it no easy task to express the music that ran in his head. But as he warmed to his task his mind would wander back to the time of his youth, and, with tightly shut eyes, he would play through one piobaireachd after another.
>
> He had received his piping lessons more than sixty years ago from an uncle in Canada, who in turn had been instructed by a Coll piper who had received his tuition from the last of the MacCrimmons – the celebrated hereditary pipers of the chiefs of the MacLeods for generations ... What the standard of playing was in that far-off time we have no means of knowing, yet it must have been a high one, for it was said that the MacCrimmons counted no pupil proficient in less than seven years.
>
> Well, the old piper has gone now, and there is none on Coll, or on Tiree either, to perpetuate the old compositions he loved so well. His tunes died with him, for some of those he played are never heard at the present day.

Seton Gordon received a very pleasant surprise over forty years later when he was judging at a piping competition. Reporting on a prize-winning player from Lewis, he commented: 'He brought out the curious melody of this ancient tune which I used to hear John Johnston of the Isle of Coll play on that island half a century ago.'

About 1936, Hector McDougall tells of when bagpipes were last played at a funeral on Coll. As the solemn funeral procession approached Crossapol beach and the graveyard came into sight at the far end of it, the piper was expected to play a lament. *Lochaber no More* was usually the tune, quite an appropriate choice given McLean's loss of the lands of Lochaber. Anyway, the funeral provisions had been rather liberally dispensed and the piper struck up with a well-known dance tune: *Miss Drummond of Perth*. So, for a long time but not forever, the funerals lost their bagpipe music.

....

Scottish dancing? – it's as easy as 1-2-3! (1) There is Scottish Country dancing which involves a group of nicely-dressed dancers, usually four couples, and each different dance progresses through a formally recognized pattern of moves. (2) Ceilidh dancing is a much less formal thing, and such is the informality of it that for a given dance there may be local variations on the moves involved. 'Every schoolboy' knows of at least two Ceilidh dances: 'The Dashing White Sergeant' and 'Strip the Willow'. (3) Highland dancing is the type that is usually seen at Highland games throughout the world, and it is mostly a competitive event performed to the accompaniment of bagpipe music. Two of the better known Highland dance names are the 'Highland Fling' and the 'Sword Dance'.

On Coll, ceilidh dances for the islanders and visitors have been a regular event for many years. In the 1930s the venue was the old school in Arinagour, and then the old village hall that was built in the 1950s began to host them. The functions took place on a Friday with a mid-evening start time but it was, of course, just a planned start time. In the summer, with long hours of daylight, the work out in the fields might still be continuing up to about 10 pm. The dance would eventually get going, with a break about 11 pm for tea and sandwiches. Finish time would be in the small hours of Saturday morning and then old and young would wend their way home not long before sunrise.

When Chrissie from the mainland married a local Coll lad, the island acquired a top-notch dancing tutor. For about three decades Chrissie introduced many of the island's children to Highland dancing, with regular teaching sessions in the old village hall. Each July, Chrissie and the dancers would leave Coll early on a Thursday to compete at the Tobermory Games. There would be whole families going to support their own dancing children, and there would be other islanders planning to see the Games but squeeze in some shopping in the town as well. Clearly, the island did not completely empty for the day – it just seemed like it – but the residue would turn out in force on the pier for the big return, mainly to see the dancing prizes and maybe to enjoy a celebratory dram from a silver cup as it was passed around the adults!

Chapter 28

War and Peace

SOUNDING rather like a season's fixtures for a Coll team there was, in times past, McLean versus McNeil, then there was McLean versus Cameron and, although not an 'own goal', there was even McLean versus McLean.

While John Garbh, the first McLean chief of Coll, was still a boy his mother remarried. McNeil of Barra, her new husband, decided to annex Coll for himself. He took the young heir to Barra and settled some of his own people onto Coll. John prepared himself for the day when he could escape from Barra and claim his rights. An account of his escape tells how a Coll galley reached Barra one night and took John on board. When his flight became known, McNeil immediately set off in pursuit with his eight-oared galley. Nearing Coll, the Barra men began to close in on their prey and it was time for the Coll men to use brains as well as brawn. They headed for a narrow channel between a steep rock and a steep part of the island's north coast. On entering it they lifted their oars and the speed of their galley carried them right through. The pursuers did not have such local knowledge and before they realised what was happening their oars on both sides were broken to pieces. To this day the narrow strait is called 'Caolas Bhristeadh Ràmh' (Sound of Breaking Oars). Ultimately, John was to regain Coll. He gathered an army from his kinsfolk on Mull and from supporters on Coll and defeated the McNeils in battle at Grishipol.

More fighting was to come when Coll was given some land in the Cameron estate at Lochaber. John, the second McLean of Coll, made it his home and he became known as John Abraich (Lochaber John). Cameron was determined to get the land back for himself and killed John in a battle at Corpach. The McLeans were never to regain the Lochaber ground.

Then, in the 16th century, McLean of Coll and McLean of Duart were quarrelling. Duart thought that Coll should support him in his own disputes, but Coll chose not to do so and as a result there were some serious feuds. When Duart decided to invade in force, their galleys were sighted and the Coll forces were quickly gathered for what became a bloody slaughter in the West End. A stream that runs here was choked with heads of the defeated – *Duart* heads – and thus it became known as Sruthan nan Ceann (Stream of the Heads).

The last major conflict on British soil was the Battle of Culloden in April 1746, and it marked the end of the Jacobite rising which is often simply called the '45. It appears that very few, if any, of Coll's islanders took up arms on the side of the 'Young Pretender', i.e. 'Bonnie Prince Charlie', and the *Culloden Papers* provide a good explanation for their stance. On 11th August 1745, Sir Alexander MacDonald wrote from Talisker on Skye to say that McLean of Coll was visiting there and had as good as promised to prevent his clan from being led astray by the 'Young Pretender'. (Mary, a daughter of McLean, had very recently married a MacLeod of Talisker.) There may have been some doubt about McLean's sincerity and Duncan Forbes of Culloden, Lord President of the Court of Session in Scotland, sent a reply to Sir Alexander about ten days later: 'My Dear Knight, I am heartily glad to hear of the wise resolution of my friend Coll. The kindred will, by his advice, I am confident, remain quiet; and will be apt to consider their chief, now at London, as an hostage for their good behaviour.'

McLean must have been allowed home from London before the Prince's last days on Scottish soil. In the autumn of 1746 a French ship was heading north to rescue the Prince and someone with local knowledge was needed to act as a navigator. Donald McLean, a seaman, was kidnapped from the Island of Tiree along with a companion, Neil McFadyen. Having made an agreement to pilot the ship in exchange for being allowed home to Tiree on the voyage south, Donald guided the ship northwards to Loch nan Uamh. With the Prince safely on board, the ship set sail on 20th September and headed out past Ardnamurchan. It passed north and west of Coll where, in the late evening light, it was sighted by a few islanders. About this time Donald realised that the ship was on a course more towards Barra and definitely not in a direction for Tiree. When it was dark enough and there were only two crewmen left on deck, Donald and Neil lowered a boat over the stern and, under rifle fire, made good their escape. They eventually made landfall at the harbour of Port-na-Luing on Coll. McLean of Coll helped the two of them to get back over to Tiree – but he kept the boat! Donald was a fugitive for nine months and then his failing health brought about his surrender. He was forced to serve two years in the government militia before being given complete freedom to return home, to marry and to raise a family. It is important to record that Prince Charles had another pilot and he was a volunteer – Donald MacLeod from Gualtergill on Skye. This Donald and the renowned Flora MacDonald were key players in the Prince's escape, but that is another story altogether.

The aftermath of Culloden was a harsh crackdown on the highland way of life, on its Gaelic tongue and the clan system. Such was the brutality after the '45 that Prince William Augustus, the youngest son of George II, is better known as Butcher Cumberland than by any royal title. However, the British Army always needed to add to its ranks, and just ten years after Culloden it was recruiting large numbers of highlanders to fight abroad. The main conflict was

The harbour at Port-na-Luing which had a small role in the '45. (Photo: E. McGee)

the Seven Years War (1754–1763), thought of by some as the first world war since there were battles in Europe and India as well as in Africa and North America.

Many Highlanders found themselves fighting in Canada, and this included forty men from Coll. There is no record of just how many, if any, of the forty ever saw the island of their birth again but, based on what happened to soldiers from other Hebridean islands, there were four possibilities: dying on the field of battle, surviving in army service, returning to civilian life in North America, or coming back home.

Moving forward to the major conflicts of the 1900s, at a recruiting station in Glasgow a young lad from Coll is going through the various procedures for enrolment in the armed forces and is asked to give his home address.

"Friesland," is the confident reply.

There is a time of uncertainty amongst the recruiting officers until it becomes clear that the lad is not referring to the Dutch province which lies about forty miles from the German border. The potential recruit is then passed on for his medical checks and questions:

"And how has your passage been today?"
"Well, it was a bit rough as usual going past Caliach Point but once the ship was inside the shelter of the Sound of Mull ..."
"No, what I meant was ..."

During the Second World War many adult males were away on service and the schoolchildren were expected to help with many of the heavy chores, such as the peat cutting. They were also expected to report on bodies and on any questionable items that were washed up on the shore. One Coll lad heard, but did not see, a plane crashing down some distance from his home and it required some persuasion before any adults took his story seriously. In their publication *Royal Air Force Connel Ferry: An Illustrated History*, Neil Owen and Phil Jones tell how in 1944 three Hurricanes on exercise out of Connel (near Oban) found themselves in poor visibility. In order to reduce the risk of collision, the pilots agreed by radio to split up. One pilot, John Stephen, was experiencing engine trouble and decided to head for Coll's emergency landing ground at Feall, but he never reached it. The Hurricane came down heavily while still some distance away and Stephen died instantly. The tragic incident was largely forgotten until Owen did some research and this led to a plaque being unveiled in August 2008, with a few of Stephen's relatives making a long journey to Coll for a very fitting commemoration event.

For part of the war there was a small RAF unit operating a listening post in the East End, and there was a small Home Guard unit with twenty-five rounds of ammunition for each man. The islanders were heavily outnumbered by rabbits, many more than the Home Guard bullets, but the bunnies became a source of fresh meat for mainland families – and a source of income to Collachs!

And now it's peace-time. Or is it always? You may be enjoying a walk along the shore and enjoying the sound of the sea lapping softly onto the beach when, out of nowhere, a pair of RAF jets suddenly appear from nowhere and scream across the island at a seemingly roof-top height.

Chapter 29

What's in a Name?

Coll – twinned with Struay?

READERS of the delightfully illustrated *Katie Morag* stories may notice some strong similarities between the real Coll and Katie's fictional Struay. However, we are only going to delve into the name of the former and there are two likely but quite different ideas as to its origin.

In Adamnan's account of the life of Saint Columba there are two relevant passages. In the first of these, Columba and his followers are sitting on '... higher ground ...' in mainland Ardnamurchan – Skene suggests their location is somewhere close to Sanna Bay. They are watching a robber whom they had encountered sailing off with his spoils, '... between the Malean [Mull] and Colosus islands.' There are divided opinions on whether Colonsay or Coll was Adamnan's Colosus, with the Rev William Reeves favouring the former and the Celtic scholar Professor William John Watson believing that it was the latter. One point here in favour of Coll is that there is high ground near Sanna Bay that would offer a view of both Mull and Coll, but Colonsay would be out of sight. The robber was not to reach his destination, since the story tells us: '... after the lapse of a few moments, a cloud arose from the sea, and caused a great hurricane, which overwhelmed him in the midst of the sea.' In the second passage Columba instructs two brethren to sail from Iona over to Mull and look for, '... a robber who came along from the island of Colosus to steal seals', and in this account Coll again has a point in its favour. The story goes on to tell how Columba was lenient, letting the man return home, and not empty-handed but with some sheep instead of seals. Soon afterwards Columba had spiritual insight of the robber's imminent death and told Baithene on Tiree to send over a sheep and some corn as last gifts. Baithene sent these immediately but then heard that the man had died suddenly the same day. The food did not go to waste – it was used at the robber's burial. A same-day scenario does fit well with neighbouring Coll.

There is also the idea that the name is derived from the old Irish Gaelic word for hazel. This thinking might be questioned on the basis that there are only a few trees and bushes on Coll, although the hazel can still be found, but the Rev Dugald MacEchern wrote in 1906 about the origin of the island's name: 'I found that the hazel had once been plentiful. Hazel nuts are found in "any amount," as the crofter will tell you, in the peat. Branches of trees and roots of various kinds are met with in the peat – often with difficulty cut by the axe and a hard black wood is found that is difficult to saw.' MacEchern also favoured Coll for Adamnan's Colosus but added: 'How it affects the derivation from hazel, I do not pretend to say.'

This etymological dissertation is now concluded with: 'Hazel and/or Colosus = Coll, but the jury is still out!'

As for the place-names within the island, Blaeu's 1654 Atlas of Scotland shows Coll with twenty-five different ones, and MacEchern estimated that at least eighty percent of these were derived from Norse. Just four of his interpretations follow:

> Anlaimh, and Loch Anlaimh (the lower mill loch) – Norse: Olaf. It would be hard to get much more Norse than that.
>
> Cornaig – Norse: Corn and vik, bay = Corn bay.
>
> Feall, and Ben Feall – Norse: fjall, a fell.
>
> Trelavaig / Trelvick – probably from Norse: troll, a troll or elf; vik, a bay = haunted bay. It is to be found on the rough bounds close to the coast between Sorisdale and Arinagour.

....

Now for surnames and forenames. There is a document dated December 1776 which lists all 938 inhabitants of the island at that time. Not surprisingly, the McLean surname is way out in front, and following it in numerical order are McDonald, McKinnon, Campbell, McPhaiden and McInnes. After all these comes a sprinkling of others.

Just thirteen different forenames account for three quarters of the population in 1776 – John, Donald, Niel (seldom the Neil spelling), Lachlane, Malcolm, Hector, Allan, Mary, Catherine, Ann, Marrion (seldom the Marion spelling), Flora, Christian. This limited selection might be considered a lack of imagination but it stems from the old tradition of naming children after their ancestors. The tradition, which has almost died away, went something like: first son named after the paternal grandfather, second son after maternal grandfather, third after father. After these, the uncles' names come into play. Daughters are similarly named after the grandmothers, the mother, and the aunts.

A ruin in the old township at Trelavaig, on the coast between Arinagour and Sorisdale. The name Trelavaig / Trelvick is probably from Norse: troll or elf; and vik, a bay = haunted bay. Haunted? Rubbish! (Photo: E. McGee)

Genealogist Tips:

http://www.scotlandspeople.gov.uk

The above is the official on-line government source of genealogical data for Scotland and it holds the Statutory Registers from 1855 onwards, the pre-1855 Old Parish Registers, Census Records; Wills & Testaments. The following advice on its use applies broadly, but the examples are mainly from Coll research work:

a) Always use the asterisk option. Searching say for a Neil McDougall? For surname enter McD* and for forename enter N*, and you will get McDougalls and McDugalls and McDonalds etc, plus Neils and Niels and Normans etc. Extra letters before the asterisk becomes a bit of trial and error. Omitting the asterisk means you may not find say 'John'. He may have normally been recorded as 'John A' or 'John Andrew', and searching for 'John*' or 'John A*' would find him, but not just 'John'.

b) It copes with the 'Mac' versus 'Mc' prefix but, for a given individual, name spelling and name variations can be inconsistent. Maybe Neil in one record and Niel in the next. Flora could be Flo/Flory/Florence, Margaret might be Peggy/Meg, Catherine could be Cath/Catharine/Kate, and so on. Surnames present a similar problem. McLean can appear as McLaine. McInnes can be McInnis/McGinnis/McGinnes. Then there are 'extreme' variations such as McLucas/McDougall, McKenzie/Mathieson and McPhaiden/McFadyen. It is worth exploring websites which have lists of forename and surname alternatives.

c) Always search for both genders. On very rare occasions there is a registration error. Plus, it can't be assumed that a 'male' name will be for a male.

d) For a time Coll and Tiree formed a joint parish and so it is as well to search across both locations, and then examine the results.

Chapter 30

Water ... of Life

Water – we will start off with brine...

'Water, water everywhere, nor any drop to drink' – some of the words in Coleridge's *Rime of the Ancyent Marinere.* On Coll we will not drink a drop of water from Tobair Nighean an Righ – the Well of the King's Daughter, maybe better known just as the 'Wishing Well'. Being sited right on the shoreline, it only ever holds sea water. The 'well' is one of the island's interesting but 'hidden' features and it is an almost circular hole about two feet in diameter and which has been worn by the sea into its smooth state over thousands of years. It is to be found on the Queen's Staircase, where a volcanic disturbance has left the basalt rocks looking almost like great steps, about seven feet long and two feet deep and wide. They form a stairway sloping gradually from the grass above the high tide line right out to sea.

Tourist Tip:

To best find and view the well, choose a time between half tide and low tide. Take the path to the right of the graveyard at Killunaig, which is on the East End road and about four miles from Arinagour. As the shore is neared, veer to the left onto the slightly higher grassy ground and follow the fence about as far as it goes. The long straight dark line of rock of the Queen's Staircase is parallel to the fence line and about twenty yards to the north-east of it. It is fairly obvious against the other lighter grey rocks. The well is near the top of the 'stair'. Caution – the 'steps' are far from being horizontal and may be quite slippery!

The Well of the King's Daughter – also known just as the Wishing Well – is to be found on the Queen's Staircase and is not far from graveyard at Killunaig. (Photo: E. McGee)

Moving on to fresh water...

Christopher Columbus would have struggled to reach the New World if his ships were not carrying enough potable water and, nowadays, when planning for astronauts to live and work in outer space it is water that is the most crucial provision to be considered. Fortunately, Coll is quite well supplied with this essential and the New Statistical Account of 1843 tells of the all the springs being '... perennial and the water pretty good for drinking'. On old maps of the island a well is identified close to every house or group of houses. In Arinagour, the old water pump still stands across the road from the shore, close to the An Cridhe footpath entrance. For many years, the villagers just had to carry the water home from the pump. Then, in the 1930s, the Arinagour houses 'got the water in' as they say, with the supply initially coming from Loch Airigh Meall Bhreide (the 'Dairy Loch').

Over the years, various means have been employed on Coll to get water to a house. In one location, a hand pump was used to bring water from a nearby well which lay below the level of the house. The pump was mounted on the kitchen wall and the cistern was directly above it in the attic. A good bit of muscle work was frequently required to keep the cistern adequately filled. Then a bright spark staying at the house on holiday noticed that the ground between it and a nearby loch did not seem to rise very much, certainly not more than 32 feet, and this was within the limit for simply siphoning the water across. All that remained was to check the quality of the water, which turned out to be satisfactory – problem solved! Some houses have resorted to bore holes. Other properties have depended on a large cistern sited on an adjacent hill-side and usually supplied by a motor-driven pump taking water from a nearby stream. One or two have found that the hydram (or hydraulic ram) is just the item to meet their needs. Perhaps not heard of this clever mechanism? The internet will tell all but, basically, the mechanism uses the flow of water in a pipe to pump a small percentage of that flow to a higher storage point. The main benefits are that no external energy supply is needed and the mechanism can run happily for decades and, as they say '24/7', with absolutely minimal maintenance.

Lastly, the water of life...

In Latin: aqua vitae. In Scottish Gaelic: uisge beatha. You may also just refer to it as whisky, or Scotch. The Rev Dr John Walker writes of there being nine distilleries operating on Coll in the 1760s. The island exported whisky as well as the surplus bear – a type of barley – which was used by the distilleries. By the 1790s the number

The old hand pump which provided water for the villagers of Arinagour sits close to the footpath entrance to *An Cridhe*. (Photo: E. McGee)

A villager on his way to (or from) the pump poses for the camera. (Photo: R. Sturgeon)

of distilleries was down to just three – and these were licensed! Licensed or unlicensed, alcohol consumption was at times a problem, for example at funerals. The Rev N. MacLean writes in 1843: 'There is one custom still prevalent which calls loudly for a reformation … drinking of ardent spirits at funerals. It is quite melancholy to consider what sums are worse than thrown away in this manner. There are instances of poor families parting with their last horse or cow, to furnish an entertainment of this kind. They reckon it a point of honour to do so.'

It is said that a few families continued to operate their own stills long after the 1822 Illicit Distillation (Scotland) Act came into force and maybe there were some on Coll, maybe even one on the stream that runs down towards the shore at Hyne. As for the quality of the home-made brand, we just don't know. We can though speculate that it might have appeared for sale on the island since any supplies from licensed distilleries on the mainland depended on a reliable cargo service. It was about the 1870s before such a service developed, and with limited security of cargo there was an element of pilfering, especially with desirable items such as whisky. What we do know is that in 1859 some travellers were taking a trip to Tiree and Coll, and they wrote an article for the Glasgow Herald, reporting that: 'on calling at the Bay of Arynagour we went up to the inn, called for a gill of whisky, which was only tasted to ascertain that it was not fit for mortals to drink.' Not exactly the water of life!

Chapter 31

TODAY AND TOMORROW

'Today' – July 2014...

Coll is once again enjoying the benefit of virtually zero light pollution. At the end of 2013 it was awarded the status of Dark Sky Community by the International Dark-Sky Association. Coll is the 22nd Dark Skies Place – in the world – and, better than that, it is the 2nd Dark Skies Community in the UK. A senior citizen tells of a time before the days of mains electricity on Coll. At the time he was a teenager and was walking along the West End road on his way back to Arinagour. It was late in the evening, with no trace of the moon and the sun had set some hours earlier. But the sky was completely clear of any haze or cloud, and so there was a simple but spectacular hemisphere above him and it was providing more than enough starlight to illuminate the road. Stars – we may safely say *millions* of them.

The island's community could now best be described as vibrant. The population, the real population of 365-days-a-year, has been steadily on the increase, recently topping two hundred and it is many a decade since that was the figure. If you're a visitor you may be confronted with rather a common question when you meet up again with your friends back home: "But what do they all do?"

Let's have a go at answering that. Firstly, very few of the islanders work anything like a '9-to-5'. There is of course farming, on the mixture of arable and grazing land. Healthy-looking cattle will be seen in plenty, but the last dairy providing milk for local consumption has long since ceased production. Don't be surprised though if there is ever a resurgence in the production of the famous Coll cheese. The humans are outnumbered by sheep, and one variety you may see of the latter is the Hebridean, a type which is small and hardy and which has a black fleece. When you see Eriskay ponies you may rest assured that you didn't board the outer isles ferry at Oban, and when you see alpacas you may rest assured that you didn't board a ship for South America. Honey is being made again – a new enterprise, but not strictly a first since there were hives on the island as early as 1762 and these were said to give a fine quality product. There is also fishing, and although it may not be on the scale imagined by Knox back in the late 1700s it has recently seen something of a small revival.

Tourism accounts for a good number of employees, especially in the summer months, and here we are talking in terms of tens rather than hundreds. The hotel, the bed & breakfast establishments, the bunk house and the other self-catering properties are often fully booked-up in the summer period.

The big employer on the island is Project Trust, accounting for about fifteen percent of the island's total population. It is a charitable organisation which was started in the late 1960s and is involved with preparing young people for voluntary work overseas. The volunteers, usually on a gap year, come to Coll for a selection course and return later for training. Providing some amusement are the rare occasions when a whole group is sitting in the ferry's lounge area, apparently oblivious to the loud tannoy message: "The vessel is now arriving at Coll. Will passengers for Coll please make their way ..." A few minutes

later on the pier, just as the ferry is preparing for departure, you may see someone running up the gangway to 'shoo' them ashore. Don't they know that next stop is Tiree and then maybe straight back to Oban? And, they're going to be sent out into the wide world!
(See: www.projecttrust.org.uk)

Then, as for many an island community, there are a number of other jobs – some voluntary – which one might expect to find:

Airfield staff – including its own fire brigade
Catering – café/hotel food and refreshments for islanders and visitors
Church
Community Centre (An Cridhe)
Cottage industries – artists, writers, etc.
Education – teaching, school meals, etc.
Emergency services – Coastguard, Fire & Rescue
Golf course – maintenance
Health service – doctor and district nurse
Petrol pumps
Pier staff – ticketing, reservations, berthing of vessels
Postal service – post office and mail delivery/collection
Recycling – includes a glass imploder
Refuse collection
Registrar – of births, deaths and marriages
Road maintenance – verges to be cut, drains and ditches to be cleared, etc.
Shop staff
Transport – school buses, taxi service, general goods to be moved
Utilities – water, telephones, electricity

When all the jobs have been taken into account, many Coll adults will boast two or more occupational hats but none may beat the record, thought to be held by a resident on the Isle of Gigha who had a claim to thirteen. Now, is there anyone upset at being missed out?

There is a thriving primary school and a pre-5 unit. The secondary school pupils mostly attend Oban High School and are able to spend weekends at home courtesy of a thirty-minute flight or, for some, by a ferry crossing.

In the village there is an excellent new community building, An Cridhe (The Heart), which was opened in 2012 by Her Royal Highness The Princess Royal. It is a multi-purpose centre, and it has an adjacent bunkhouse.

Tomorrow?

Originally there was no intention of suggesting in this book how Coll might change and develop in the coming years. For Coll, there did not appear to be a list of profound predictions such as the words of the Brahan Seer. But, if not actually prophesying, then perhaps a few ideas may be permitted here:

1) A faster ferry crossing? Travellers in the Channel Islands, in the Canaries, in the Mediterranean, and in other parts of the world, are experiencing ferries moving at twenty-five knots and more. But maybe it is the sea conditions to the west of Mull that are a stumbling block to speeds much in excess of today's seventeen knots.

2) An indicator board on the top of Ben Hogh? You know the sort of thing – a circular plate mounted firmly about chest height and with a number of etched lines, radiating from the centre and pointing to the main landmarks such as islands, mountain tops, lighthouses. With place-names on it, of course.

3) A distillery? Just a thought, from a non-whisky drinker. There used to be *nine*, but presumably each was very small.

Then, there was great excitement during some property renovation on the island in 2007. What should surface in the middle of it but a newspaper item clearly dated AD 2032 and depicting a 'skyscraper' metropolis whose scale would certainly put Arinagour in the shade, and maybe even dwarf Oban. The newspaper had been used as a lining material on the walls and had been covered over with other paper and paint. The main fragment and some smaller pieces which all seemed to be from the same source were given the kind of careful handling as would befit the Dead Sea scrolls. As the pieces were drying out there was no obvious sign of a scrap containing the rest of the date, i.e. the day and month. The one outstanding problem now is to find the relevant expertise which will give the puzzle its due attention and not to have it handled on the present 'Mañana' basis.

Mañana? At an international conference on languages, a professor of Scottish Gaelic and a professor of Spanish get to know one another during a break:

> "Tell me this Angus. What word do you have in Gaelic for 'Mañana'?"
>
> "Och Manuel, that iss easy. You see, over the many, many centuries of our most beautiful language – and they say that it wass the language of the Garden of Eden – we haff neffer effer found the need for a word that expresses such urgency."

Tomorrow, on Coll? What's the rush? Do come and see for yourself.

A piece of newspaper dated AD 2032. It was uncovered in 2007 during restoration of an old house on Coll, and it had been used as lining paper on a wall. (Photo: E. McGee)

Bibliography

An Iodhlann, *Island of Two Harvests – A Historical Guide to the Island of Tiree* (2003)

Anderson, George & Peter, *Guide to the Highlands and Islands of Scotland – Third Edition* (Adam & Charles Black, 1851)

Anderson, Iain F., *To Introduce the Hebrides* (Herbert Jenkins, 1933)

Anderson, William, *The Scottish Nation* (Fullarton, 1853)

Barron, Evan MacLeod, *Prince Charlie's Pilot; a Record of Loyalty and Devotion* (Public domain)

Beveridge, Erskine, *Coll and Tiree: Their Prehistoric Forts and Ecclesiastical Antiquities* (Edinburgh University Press, 1903/facsimile edition by Birlinn, 2000)

Bowler & Hunter, *Birds of Tiree and Coll* (Paircwood Publishing, 2007)

Bowler, Grant, Self & Wellock, *Wild Flowers of Coll and Tiree* (Cinquefoil Publishing, 2008)

Crawford, John, *Archaeological collections from sand-hill sites in the Isle of Coll, Argyll & Bute* (1997)

Dasent, George Webbe, *The Story of Burnt Njal*, (Written in the 13th century in Icelandic and translated by Dasent in the 19th century)

Duckworth & Langmuir, *West Highland Steamers – Second Edition* (Richard Tilling, 1950)

Forbes, Duncan George, of Culloden – *Culloden Papers* (Cadell and Davies, 1815)

Gibson, John Graham, *Old and New World Highland Bagpiping* (McGill-Queen's Press, 2002)

Gregory, Donald, *History of the Western Highlands and Isles of Scotland from A.D. 1493 to A.D. 1625 with a Brief Introductory Sketch from A.D. 30 to A.D. 1493* (William Tait, Edinburgh, 1836)

Gregory, Donald & Iona Club, *Collectanea de Rebus Albanicis: Consisting of Original Papers and Documents relating to the history of the Highlands and Islands of Scotland* (Thomas G. Stevenson, Edinburgh, 1847)

Haggard, H. Rider, *A Farmer's Year for 1898* (Longmans, Green & Co., 1906)

Haswell-Smith, Hamish, *The Scottish Islands* (Canongate Books, 1996)

Hedderwick, Mairi, *The Last Laird of Coll* (Birlinn, 2011)

Hughes, Mike, *The Hebrides at War* (Canongate Books Ltd, 1998)

Hutchison, Iain, *Air Ambulance: Six Decades of the Scottish Air Ambulance Service* (Kea Publishing, 1996)

Innes, Nelson, *The Antiquities Ecclesiastical and Territorial of the Parishes of Scotland* (Lizars, 1854)

Johnson, Samuel & Boswell, James, *Journey to the Hebrides* (Canongate Books, 1996)

Knox, John, *A Tour through the Highlands of Scotland and the Hebride Isles in 1786* (J. Walter, Charing-Cross, 1787)

Lawson, Rev Roderick, *A Flight to St Kilda* (Parlane, 1902)

Logie, David W., *An Account of a Trip from Stirling to St Kilda in the s.s. "Hebridean" of Glasgow* (1889)

Lord, Richard, *Impression Bay – Convict Probation Station to Civilian Quarantine Station* (Richard Lord and Partners, 1992)

Lumsden, James, *Lumsden & Son's Steam-boat Companion or Stranger's Guide to the Western Isles & Highlands of Scotland* (1839)

Lunghi, Martin, *Eilean Cholla – a Guide to the Hebridean Isle of Coll* (Toad Wine Press, 2000)

MacBain, Alex., *Place Names Highlands & Islands of Scotland* (Eneas MacKay, 1922)

MacCulloch, John, *The Highlands and Western Isles of Scotland – Annual Journeys between 1811 and 1821 – in Letters to Sir Walter Scott, Bart.*, (Longman, 1824)

MacDonald, James, *General View of the Agriculture of the Hebrides* (R. Phillips, 1811)

MacDougall, Betty, *Folklore from Coll* (1978)

MacDougall, Betty, *Guide to Coll* (1986)

MacDougall, Hector & Cameron, Rev Hector, *Handbook to the Islands of Coll and Tiree* (Archibald Sinclair, 1937)

MacEchern, Rev Dugald, *Transactions of the Gaelic Society of Inverness Volume XXIX 1914–1919*, although MacEchern's article was actually written in 1906.

MacKay, James, *The St Kilda Steamers: A History of McCallum, Orme & Co.* (Tempus Publishing, 2006)

MacKay, James A., *Islands Postal History Series No. 9 – Mull, Iona, Coll and Tiree* (MacKay, 1979)

McLean, J.P., *A History of the Clan McLean* (Robert Clarke & Co., 1889)

McLean, J.P., *An Account of the Surname McLean from the Manuscript of 1751 and a Sketch of the Life and Writings of Lachlan McLean* (Aldine Publishing House – Ohio, 1914)

McLean, J.P., *A Renaissance of the Clan MacLean* (Columbus, Ohio, 1913)

McLean, Lachlan, *Adhamh agus Eubh* (MacLachlan & Stewart, 1837)

McNeill, Murdoch, *Colonsay – One of the Hebrides* (David Douglas, 1910)

MacRae, Alexander, *Revivals in the Highlands and Islands in the 19th Century* (Tentmaker Publications, 1998)

Maidment, James, *Spottiswoode Miscellany – a Collection of Original Papers and Tracts – Volume II* (Spottiswoode Society, 1845)

Martin, Martin – see: Monro, Donald

Menzies, Lucy, *Saint Columba of Iona* (J. M. Dent & Sons, 1920)

Mithen, Steven, *To the Islands* (2010, Two Ravens Press)

Monro, Donald, *Description of the Occidental i.e. Western Isles of Scotland* – Monro's 1549 work is included with *A Description of the Western Isles of Scotland Circa 1695* by Martin (Birlinn, 1999)

Muir, Thomas Scott, *Ecclesiological Notes on Some of the Islands of Scotland* (David Douglas, 1885)

Murray, Sarah, *Companion and Useful Guide to the Beauties in the Western Highlands of Scotland, and in the Hebrides* (G. & W. Nicol, 1803)

Necker de Saussure, Professor Louis Albert, *Voyage to the Hebrides* (Phillips & Co., London, 1822)

Ogg, Diana, *Coll – Island of the Hebrides* (Dryad Press 1988)

Ogg, John, *House in the Hebrides* (Cowrie Press, 2004)

Otter, Rev William, *The Life and Remains of Edward Daniel Clarke* (George Cowie and Co., 1825)

Owen, Neil & Jones, Phil, *Royal Air Force Connel Ferry: An Illustrated History*

Pennant, Thomas, *A Tour in Scotland 1769* (Benj. White, 1776)

Reeves, William (bishop), *The Life of St. Columba, Founder of Hy; written by Adamnan, ninth abbot of that monastery* (Irish Archaeological and Celtic Society, 1857)

Richards, Eric, *A History of the Highland Clearances* (Taylor & Francis, 1982)

Robins, Nicholas and Meek, Donald E., *The Kingdom of MacBrayne* (Birlinn, 2006)

Scott, Hew, *Fasti Ecclesiæ Scoticanæ – The Succession of Ministers in the Church of Scotland from the Reformation* (Oliver and Boyd, 1923)

Sinclair, Rev A. Mclean, *The Clan Gillean* (Haszard and Moore, 1899)

Skene, William, *Celtic Scotland: A History of Ancient Alban Vol III – Land and People* (Douglas, 1890)

Spurkland, Terje, *Norwegian Runes and Runic Inscriptions* (Translation by Betsy van der Hoek published by the Boydell Press, 2005)

Thomson, Derick, *Why Gaelic matters* (Saltire Society / An Comunn Gaidhealach 1984)

Thomson, Robert, *A Cruise in the Western Hebrides* or *A Week on Board the s.s. "Hebridean"* (1891, printed by A. Cochrane, Glasgow)

Thomson, William, *A tour in England and Scotland in 1785* (Robinson, 1788)

Walker, Rev Dr John, *Report on the Hebrides of 1764 and 1771* – Edited by Margaret M. McKay (John Donald, 1980)

Weyndling, Walter, *Ferry Tales of Argyll and the Isles* (Birlinn, 2003)

Other sources – the websites and/or some editions and proceedings of the following newspapers, periodicals and organisations:

Argyll & Bute Council
British Archaeology
Caledonian Mercury
Celtic Monthly: a Magazine for Highlanders
Clyde Cruising Club
Coll Magazine
Daily Express
Evening Times (of Glasgow)
General Assembly of the Free Church of Scotland
Glasgow Courant
Glasgow Herald
Hansard
Highland and Agricultural Society of Scotland
Inverness Journal
Morning Chronicle
National Geographic Magazine
NATS (National Air Traffic Services)
Oban Times
Observer
A 1932 copy had been used as lining paper. It included a *Vitaglass* windows advert, 'designed to last for a century', i.e. to 2032 AD.
People's Journal
Pigots Directory
Press & Journal
RNLI – Royal National Lifeboat Institution
RCAHMS – Royal Commission on the Ancient and Historical Monuments of Scotland
RSPB – Royal Society for the Protection of Birds
SCAPE Trust – Scottish Coastal Archaeology and the Problem of Erosion
Scotsman
Scottish Highlander
Scottish Invertebrate News
SSPCK – Society in Scotland for Propagating Christian Knowledge
Statistical Accounts of Scotland

- Tiree and Coll, the Old Account, of 1791–99, by Reverend A. McColl
- Tiree and Coll, the New Account, of 1834–45, by Reverend N. McLean

Sydney Herald (Australia)
The Times

Acknowledgements

For their help in bringing this book into being, my sincere thanks go to some individuals and groups of people:

a) The NHS – the National Health Service – (and why not?) for diagnosing my nasty pneumonia in 2007. That gave me good cause to have a period of convalescence on some Hebridean island, where, thanks to Fiona Kennedy, the seed of an idea was sown. That idea became a labour of love and, finally, a book.

b) Collachs everywhere, for their photographs, advice, documents, press clippings, stories, etc. Collach? – a rather loose definition is someone born and brought up on the island; or someone who perhaps came ashore to fix a loose slate, immediately fell in love with the island and never left it; or maybe even a second (or third, or fourth, etc) generation descendant now living in some far-flung corner of the world.

c) Staff at the following sites, for their help with my search for information: National Library of Scotland, National Archives of Scotland, Hunterian Museum, Mitchell Library in Glasgow, Stirling Libraries, Oban Times office, University of Glasgow Archive Services, An Iodhlann (Tiree's historical centre).

d) My wife and family for their patience and support throughout, and for proof reading.

e) Her Royal Highness The Princess Royal for providing an excellent foreword.

f) Alayne Barton and the Islands Book Trust, for just about everything else – and 'everything' was a lot.

Some Coll photos have been copied and passed around, occasionally making it difficult to give credit to the photographer or to name the owner. In addition to my own and my relatives' photos, those in the book are from a variety of collections. One or two seem to be in the public domain. Since one aim of the book is to financially help the Coll community, and not to line my pockets, I will hopefully be forgiven for any omissions or for any incorrect acknowledgement.

Ewen McGee
August 2014

THE ISLANDS BOOK TRUST – high quality books on island themes in English and Gaelic

Based in Lewis, the Islands Book Trust are a charity committed to furthering understanding and appreciation of the history of Scottish islands in their wider Celtic and Nordic context. We do this through publishing books, organising talks and conferences, visits, radio broadcasts, research and education on island themes. For details of membership of the Book Trust, which will keep you in touch with all our publications and other activities, see www.theislandsbooktrust.com, phone 01851 830316, or visit us at the address below where a good selection of our books is available.

The Islands Book Trust, Laxay Hall, Laxay, Isle of Lewis, HS2 9PJ

Tel: 01851 830316

www.theislandsbooktrust.com

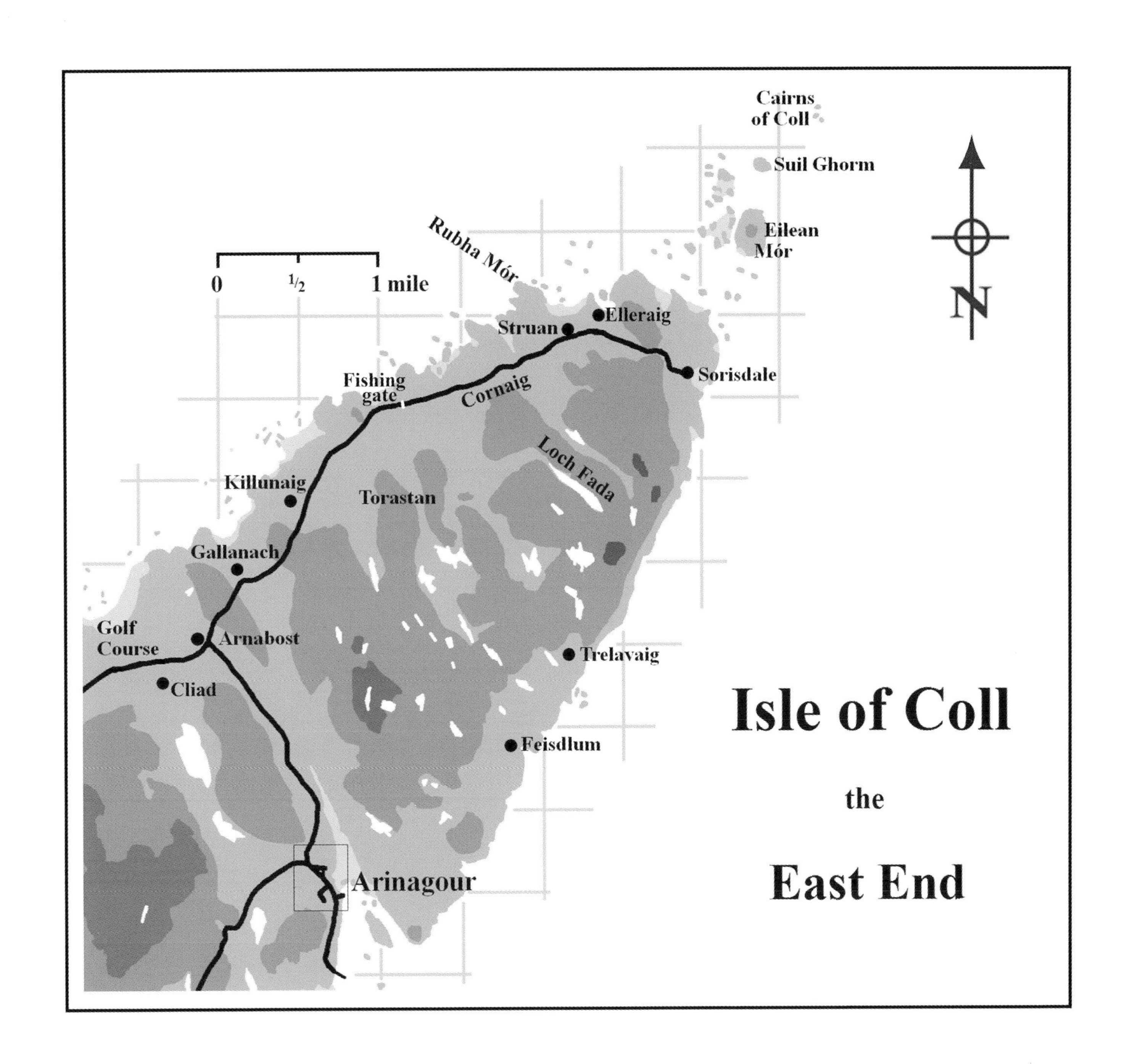

Cairns
of Coll
Suil Ghorm
Eilean
Mór
Rubha Mór
N
0
1/2
1 mile
Struan
Elleraig
Sorisdale
Fishing
gate
Cornaig
Loch Fada
Killunaig
Torastan
Gallanach
Golf
Course
Arnabost
Cliad
Trelavaig
Feisdlum
Arinagour
Isle of Coll
the
East End